Designing Democracy

Hans Gersbach

Designing Democracy

Ideas for Better Rules

Springer

Professor Dr. Hans Gersbach
University of Heidelberg
Alfred Weber Institute for Economics
Grabengasse 14
69117 Heidelberg
Germany

Cataloging-in-Publication Data applied for

A catalog record for this book is available from the Library of Congress.

Bibliographic information published by Die Deutsche Bibliothek
Die Deutsche Bibliothek lists this publication in the Deutsche Nationalbibliografie; detailed bibliographic data available in the internet at *http://dnb.ddb.de*

ISBN 3-540-22402-5 Springer Berlin Heidelberg New York

Springer is a part of Springer Science+Business Media
springeronline.com

Cover design: Erich Kirchner, Heidelberg
Production: Helmut Petri
Printing: betz-druck

SPIN 11298984 Printed on acid-free paper – 43/3130 – 5 4 3 2 1 0

Preface

While liberal democracies are the best systems of self-governance for societies, they rarely invoke great enthusiasm. On the one hand, democracies have been known to fail in achieving efficient or fair allocations. On the other hand, many citizens take the democratic system for granted as they have yet to experience an alternative.

In this book the vision we propose is that the potential of democracies has not yet been exhausted, and that optimal democracies are both the utopia for societies and the aim that scientists should be committed to.

We present a number of ideas for drawing up new rules to improve the functioning of democracies. The book falls into two parts.

The first part examines ways of combining incentive contracts with democratic elections. We suggest that a judicious combination of these two elements as a dual mechanism can alleviate a wide range of political failures, while at the same time adhering to the founding principles of democracies.

The second part presents new rules for decision-making and agenda setting. Together with modern communication devices, these rules can sometimes transcend the limitations of liberal democracies in achieving desirable outcomes. Examples of such rules include the flexible majority rule where the size of the majority required depends on the proposal, or the rule that only those belonging to the winning majority can be taxed.

At this stage, the scope and utility of these suggestions cannot be fully estimated. However, we hope that the ideas presented will at least to some extent revive an interest in the democratic system and an appreciation of its potentials.

I take great pleasure in expressing my thanks to many friends and colleagues who have helped me critically assess the ideas. Peter Bernholz, Ulrich Erlenmaier, Volker Hahn, Hans Haller, and Verena Liessem challenged the models and arguments presented in this book and prompted me to rethink the main implication of this work. I benefitted from discussions at the annual meetings of the European Public Choice Society, the Econometric and European Economic Association, the German Economic Association, at seminars on my tour of California (Universities of Los Angeles, Davis, Irvine, and San Diego) and at seminars in Basel, Leuven, Mannheim, and Rotterdam. I am deeply grateful for various comments and help along the way from Alexandrina Braack, Clive Bell, Jürgen Eichberger, Amihai Glazer, Hans-Peter Grüner, Martin Hellwig, Mark Machina, Wolfgang Merkel, Thomas Petersen, Till Requate, Annette Schiller, Manfred Schmidt, Armin Schmutzler, Otto Swank, and Eva Terberger. Finally, I would also like to thank Andrew Jenkins, Markus Müller, and Michael Neumann for their excellent research assistance.

Heidelberg, August 2004 *Hans Gersbach*

Contents

Part I. Incentive Contracts and Elections

Part II. Rules for Decision-Making and Agenda Setting

Part I

Incentive Contracts and Elections

1. Overview

1.1 The Ideas

In the first part we suggest that the judicious combination of incentive contracts and democratic elections might alleviate a range of potential inefficiencies in democratic decision-making without impairing the essence of democracies, such as equal agenda and voting rights, freedom of speech, and free formation of political parties. We present four broad ideas on how the dual mechanism - contracts and elections - may be used to overcome shortcomings in democracies.

- *Short-termism and long-term policies*

Many efficient policies have an investment characteristic for voters with short-term costs, while the benefits accrue after future elections. Examples include the pressing issue of unemployment in Europe or environmental protection.

Often, voters may not be able to motivate politicians to invest in long-term beneficial projects, because future benefits for society have little bearing on elections today. The dual mechanism can help to solve such underinvestment problems.

The combination of incentive contracts and elections takes the following form. If a politician wishes to stand for reelection or if he is successfully reelected, he must accept that his future income or utility is dependent on future developments in the society. For instance, if his policies generate long-term benefits for society, a politician may receive special monetary remunerations in the distant future, or he may become a special honorary citizen.

We consider two scenarios in which long-term contracts coupled with democratic elections can align the interests of politicians and voters. In the first case, voters cannot immediately distinguish between the types of policies undertaken and try to infer them from the information available. In the second case, the type of policy is known to the voters, but they may be faced with asymmetric information regarding the types of politicians. In this case, we also allow politicians to offer incentive contracts themselves during their campaigns.

- *Randomness of elections, credible communication, and reelection thresholds*

The randomness of future election outcomes may not provide politicians with sufficient motivation to devote a socially desirable amount of effort to certain tasks. For example, when voter preferences shift, sanctions or rewards created by elections are insufficient to motivate politicians to act in the interest of voters. The politician then has an incentive to choose the effort allocation according to his own preferences.

During campaigns, however, politicians may promise policies that, once they are in office, lack sufficient incentives for their implementation, thus depriving these promises of credibility. We suggest that adding threshold incentive contracts to the election mechanism can make communication credible between politicians and the public during campaigns and provide socially desirable incentives. A threshold contract stipulates the minimum performance level a politician must achieve in order to have the right to stand for reelection. At first, these contracts may appear to worsen the problem that politicians are often unrewarded for their efforts, as their probability of remaining in office decreases. However, when reelection chances are uncertain, social welfare can be increased through the incentive contract, as deviations toward lower effort are punished more heavily.

The threshold incentive contract is equivalent to a conditional term limit imposed by a court or by the candidate himself. Thus, it does not diminish the scope of the fundamental liberal democratic principle of free and anonymous elections. Finally (and relying more on intuitive arguments than on models), more credible communication would be helpful in avoiding public discontent with the political process. This effect is desirable for the very long-term perspectives democracies should have.

- *Effort incentives and monetary rewards*

Democratic societies use elections and reelections to motivate politicians to invest effort in accordance with the desires of the voters. This can make for a challenging motivation problem, because the outcomes of tasks may be difficult to measure and observe. Whereas the consequences of combatting unemployment or the consequences of crime prevention measures can be derived from a time series of a single number, the outcome of a reform of the health-care system is not measurable in simple figures, or with any high degree of precision.

We show that elections cannot provide sufficient incentives to implement the socially optimal solution when the benefits from a politician's effort are sufficiently noisy. We suggest that it is beneficial to add an incentive contract that the politician must accept in order to stand for reelection, even if all possible information about the performance of the politician is available to voters at the election date. An incentive contract stipulates the wages the politician receives in the first and second period, as long as he is in office. The combination of elections and an incentive contract for the politician leads to a socially optimal effort level.

- *Selection of candidates and wage costs*

While we can offer simple models to support our ideas, we also provide an example for the limitations of incentive contracts. The counter-example rests on externalities when candidates incur private costs from holding office but may wish to avoid undesirable policies by standing for election.

We consider two scenarios. In the first case, candidates for the executive or the legislative branch can offer a wage contract during campaigns that becomes effective upon election and determines their remuneration in the first term. In the second scenario, the public determines the remuneration of politicians in advance. We show that competitive wage offers by candidates lead to lower social welfare than remunerations predetermined by the public, since less competent candidates are elected, or wage costs are higher.

1.2 The Theme

The combination of incentive contracts and elections represents a set of novel institutional rules in modern democracies. These rules require constitutional changes. The dual mechanism aims at alleviating political failure without impairing the foundation of democracies. Our proposal is related to several strands in the literature and is indebted to different schools of thought.

First, research has demonstrated the existence of policy failures in a variety of circumstances. Comprehensive surveys and discussions can be found in the classical work by Buchanan and Tullock (1965), and in Olson (1965, 1982), Niskanen (1971), Tollison (1982), Frey (1983), Stiglitz and Heertje (1989), Mueller (1989), Bernholz and Breyer (1993), Dixit (1995), Drazen (2000), and Persson and Tabellini (2000).

The existence and importance of political failures can be disputed. This argument has been thoroughly developed by Wittman (1995). Moreover, Bernholz (1997, 1999) indicates how a political Coase theorem can be formulated that may diminish the importance of impossibility theorems in social choice, such as the Arrow (1951) impossibility theorem and the Sen (1970) theorem on the impossibility of a Paretian liberal. For our purposes, we begin with the premise that political failures cannot be excluded *a priori*, and therefore neither the optimism portrayed by a political Coase theorem nor the pessimism of most of the public choice literature applies universally.

Moreover, the notion of a political failure itself is highly controversial. Refraining from an engagement with this long-standing debate, we use the terms "social returns" and "social welfare" throughout the book. For most of our ideas, this welfare criterion is not controversial. Moreover, it is usually sufficient to associate "socially preferred" with "preferred by a majority of voters".

Second, our discussion is closely related to the normative branch of political economy summarized in recent books by Drazen (2000) and Persson and Tabellini (2000). In our work, we share the view that institutional arrangements matter, but we broaden the range of feasible democratic institutions by our combination of incentive contracts and elections.

Third, incentive contracts are often used abundantly in private firms and public organizations. For instance, there is a rapidly growing body of literature on incentive contracts for central bankers. The government imposes a penalty if it can verify that the central bank has not attempted to meet its target level.[1] We go further and combine the democratic decision-making process with incentive contracts.[2]

It is important to stress that incentive contracts should complement a liberal democracy, but not substitute it. Hence, we only consider a restricted set of admissible contracts in this part. The restrictions are the foundations of liberal democracies and standard measurability and verifiability constraints in contract design.

[1] For the theory of the enforcement of such arrangements and the nature of penalties, see Persson and Tabellini (1993), Walsh (1995a), Walsh (1995b), Lockwood (1997), Svensson (1997), and Jensen (1997).

[2] Incentive contracts for politicians are not allowed in modern democracies. Historically, contracts were used to limit the power of rulers. In the Middle Ages specific contracts for rulers were a step for the development of constitutions or a mean to commit them to pursue certain policies (e.g. Kleinheyer (1968), Vierhaus (1977), Pozza (1997), and Lottes (2000)). Moreover, in ancient Athens, the officials were liable with their personal funds. In some cases officials were even executed in case the assembly of citizens was not satisfied with their performance (see e.g. Bleicken (1991)).

In future research, it will be necessary to embed the dual mechanism in more sophisticated models. Such models incorporating voter heterogeneity are available in many varieties, and go back to the pioneering work of Downs (1957) and Black (1958) (see surveys and contributions by Enelow and Hinich (1984), Mueller (1989), Bernholz and Breyer (1993), Alesina and Rosenthal (1995), Drazen (2000), and Persson and Tabellini (2000)). Moreover, it will be necessary to explore the role of intrinsic motivation of politicians and contractual and communication barriers to the introduction of incentive contracts in greater depth. Finally, it will be important to broaden the perspective in order to allow for alternative institutional arrangements (see e.g. Lohmann (2003)) and different types of democracies (see e.g. Lipset (1995), Schmidt (2000), Merkel et al. (2003)). Nevertheless, current work by the author and co-authors (see e.g. Liessem (2002) and Gersbach and Kleinschmidt (2004)) suggests that the dual mechanism has potential.

We have organized Part One as follows: In chapters 2 and 3, we consider how the combination of incentive contracts and elections can encourage politicians to adopt long-term, socially desirable policies. In the fourth chapter, we examine threshold incentive contracts. In the fifth chapter, we examine the combination of incentive contracts and elections for a task with short-term, noisy consequences. In the final chapter, we examine a potential limitation to the combination of elections and contracts.

2. Unobservability and Short-Termism in Long-Term Policies[1]

2.1 Introduction

In this chapter we consider how democracies can induce that long-term beneficial policies are undertaken by politicians, if policies are not observable at the time of election. In such circumstances, voters cannot provide appropriate incentives by reelection decisions to motivate politicians to implement long-term beneficial policies.

A typical example of a long-term policy is the pressing issue of unemployment in Europe. Reforming the labor market is generally considered inevitable in order to remedy unemployment. However, introducing labor market reforms may initially cause disruptions and even higher unemployment because some layoffs will occur immediately, while the creation of new jobs may take time. Similar patterns manifest themselves in the transition phases from centrally planned economies towards market economies involving disorganization which lowers temporarily GDP. Or, investments in infrastructure may require immediate consumer sacrifices from voters whereas the returns only accrue later.

We examine how politicians can be motivated to pursue policies displaying such an investment or down-up characteristic by us-

[1] A previous version of this chapter has appeared in Gersbach (2003).

ing the dual system of incentive contracts and elections. Elections will leave the power to select the politicians with the voters. But politicians aiming at being reelected must adopt an incentive contract that makes their income or further reelection contingent on future macroeconomic performance such as GDP, unemployment or levels of socially damaging emissions. As an example we choose GDP.

We consider a model in which an elected politician faces the following options. First, he can undertake a socially desirable investment or down-up policy, i.e. a policy where the expected long-term benefits outweigh the short-term costs in GDP. Second, he can adopt a short-term policy which increases welfare temporarily but involves considerable GDP losses in the future. Third, he can choose to do nothing and continue with the status quo. The politician will derive some private benefits if projects yield social returns above the status quo. The overall utility of the politician increases with the probability of being reelected as well as with the expected private net returns from his policy decisions.

Voters observe the developments of GDP and try to infer the type of policies from those data. Since voters cannot immediately distinguish between a policy with investment characteristic, a short-term policy or the status quo, they face a serious inference problem at the reelection stage. If they observe economic stagnation, they do not know whether this has been caused by the politician having done nothing or having invested in the future.

In such circumstances voters cannot provide appropriate incentives by reelection decisions to motivate politicians to implement down-up policies. If they never reelect policy makers, the incentive for the incumbent to undertake short-term policies is high because he will not be reelected anyway and he derives private benefits from the short-term policy. If voters automatically reelect the incumbent, he has no incentive for investment policies either because he gets reelected anyway and again, he can derive private benefits from short-term policies without negative consequences. If voters reelect incumbents performing well in the past period, politicians will adopt short-term policies because such policies will increase welfare in the election period itself. In all events, voters cannot provide appropriate incentives for politicians to adopt socially optimal down-up policies by their reelection decisions.

In this chapter we suggest that the combination of incentive contracts and elections can motivate politicians seeking reelection to pursue socially desirable down-up policies. If a politician wants to stand for reelection, he must be willing to accept that his future income is dependent on macroeconomic variables.

The chapter is organized as follows: In the next section, we outline the model and our assumptions. In section 2.3, we consider the potentialities and limitations of the reelection mechanism in achieving optimal decisions. In section 2.4, we show that appropriate incentive contracts can yield socially optimal decisions. Then we discuss how such contracts can be designed and enforced. In section 2.5, we discuss how the dual mechanism might solve other inefficiencies in politics. Then we discuss practical issues in section 2.6. Section 2.7 presents our conclusions.

2.2 The Model

We analyze a dynamic game with two periods (terms). For simplicity, we assume that the politician (or agent) whose decisions we are analyzing is risk-neutral. The net benefits (or net cost if negative) a policy generates for the public are denoted by V, indexed by the type of the project and by the time period. The game is as follows:

Stage 1: At the beginning of period 1, the public decides on the reelection scheme for a politician in office. According to this reelection scheme the politician will be reelected or dismissed in stage 3. We use p $(0 \leq p \leq 1)$ to denote the probability that the politician will be reelected. p will in general depend on first-period returns V^1.

Stage 2: The agent must decide whether to undertake certain projects in period 1. He has three options. He can undertake a short-term policy (STP) which generates a positive return $V_S^1 > 0$ in this period, but a negative return $V_S^2 < 0$ in the next period. The second option is a long-term policy (LTP). The long-term policy has uncertain short-term consequences V_L^{1i} with i either High (H) or Low (L). We assume that $V_L^{1H} = V_S^1$ and $V_L^{1L} = 0$. LTP generates positive payoffs $V_L^2 > 0$ in the next period. The *a priori* probability for value V_L^{1i} is π_i. The final option for the policymaker is to continue with the status quo and to do nothing (NOT). Payoffs in this case in both periods are $V_N^1 = 0$ and $V_N^2 = 0$, respectively.

The agent decides among his options $\{STP, LTP, NOT\}$.

Stage 3: Returns of the first period are revealed. The public decides on the reelection of the politician for the second period according to the election scheme chosen in stage 1.

The assumption $V_L^{1H} = V_S^1$ implies that voters cannot distinguish between LTP and STP at the reelection stage. The assumption $V_L^{1L} = 0$ makes it impossible for voters to distinguish LTP from the status quo NOT.[2]

There are many examples of LTP projects versus STP or NOT projects. We have already mentioned labor market reforms or transition processes from centrally planned economies towards market economies. In some cases, STP might be interpreted as overspending in the popular notion of pork-barrel politics as explored in Weingast (1981) and Inman and Fitts (1990). Other examples are political business cycles, where politicians adopt short-term policies instead of long-term policies before elections leading to upturns before and downturns after elections.[3]

We assume that a politician can generate private returns if he realizes project returns above the status quo as long as he is in power. If he is in power and realizes a project return V for the

[2] This assumption is consistent with the rational ignorance concept widely discussed in the public choice literature (see Mueller (1989) and Bernholz and Breyer (1993) for surveys). It is also consistent with retrospective voting behavior where voters evaluate politicians by their performance in the last period.

[3] The literature on political business cycles started with Nordhaus (1975) and Ben-Porath (1975), complemented by ideological business cycles in Hibbs (1977). The theory has been adapted to incorporate rational expectations and information asymmetries in Rogoff (1990), Cukierman and Meltzer (1986), Hibbs (1992) and Persson and Tabellini (1993).

public in a particular period, we assume that his private benefits are given by:

$$\alpha \max[V, 0] \tag{2.1}$$

where α is some number $0 < \alpha < 1$. Therefore total project returns are $V + \alpha V$ if $V > 0$ and V if $V < 0$. $V_S^1 = V_L^{1H}$, V_S^2 and V_L^2 represent the returns which accrue fully to voters. This simplifies the exposition. The above assumption is justified by the observation that high returns enable the agent to channel some returns to interest groups that support him, as is suggested by the large body of literature on public choice. The assumption appears to be more restrictive than needed. Any discrepancy between welfare and private returns, e.g. differences in the discount rates or different policy preferences, will generate the similar inefficiencies issues discussed in this chapter.

We concentrate on the agent's utility in period 1, when he stands for reelection. Utility increases both with the probability that the public will reelect the agent and with the present value of the expected private net returns from his policy decisions. Expected private returns from policies over both periods are denoted by R. Note that R itself depends on the probability p of being reelected and thus on the probability of whether returns in the second period can be realized by the politician. p represents the strategy space of the public. We assume that utility is given by

$$U = mR + (1 - m)p. \tag{2.2}$$

The parameter m, with $0 < m < 1$, is the weight the agent assigns to private returns compared to the weight he assigns to the benefits from holding office which themselves depend on the chances of being reelected.[4] The utility from holding office may depend on monetary benefits, such as a fixed wage, and on non-monetary benefits, such as prestige or the desire for a statesman-like image. A value for m close to 1 means that the agent is mainly motivated by the policies he implements. A low value for m means that the agent is mainly concerned about holding office.

We denote the expected returns from the options STP, LTP and NOT by EV_S, EV_L, and EV_N, respectively. Thus:

$$EV_S = V_S^1 + \delta\, V_S^2$$
$$EV_L = \pi_H\, V_L^{1H} + (1-\pi_H)\, V_L^{1L} + \delta\, V_L^2 = \pi_H V_S^1 + \delta\, V_L^2$$
$$EV_N = V_N^1 + \delta\, V_N^2 = 0.$$

δ is the discount factor $(0 < \delta \leq 1)$. The discount factor is assumed to be the same for the public and the politicians. We assume that

$$EV_L > EV_N > EV_S$$
$$V_S^1 > EV_L.$$

The first of the preceding assumptions immediately implies that the socially optimal policy is LTP. If the public cannot observe the actual decisions of politicians, it has to infer the policies from the realization of returns in this period. However, since $V_L^{1H} = V_S^1$ and $V_L^{1L} = V_N^1 = 0$, such inference is limited, because there is no way of distinguishing LTP from STP or LTP from NOT.

[4] Obviously, using R and p in a utility function is delicate and only a shortcut for a true intertemporal utility representation which will be introduced in the next chapter.

2.3 Fixed and Conditional Reelection Probabilities

In this section, we consider how the reelection mechanism works in our model. In order to give the reelection mechanism the best chance of motivating a politician to embark on socially beneficial long-term projects, we assume that voters can commit themselves to a particular reelection strategy at the beginning of the election. We are looking for a subgame perfect Nash equilibrium consisting of a reelection function $p(V^1)$ and an investment decision by the politician. As we will see, no matter which reelection scheme is chosen, the politician will never adopt LTP. This result holds even more in a more realistic scenario in which the voters cannot commit themselves to a particular reelection strategy at the beginning of a term.

We first ask whether a fixed reelection probability can induce the politician to invest in LTP. As the following proposition demonstrates, the answer is no:

Proposition 2.1

For any fixed p $(0 \leq p \leq 1)$*, the politician chooses* STP*.*

Proof

The utility from STP is given by

$$U(STP) = m\,\alpha\,V_S^1 + (1-m)p. \tag{2.3}$$

If the politician selects LTP he obtains

$$\begin{aligned} U(LTP) &= m\{\alpha\,\pi_H\,V_S^1 + \alpha\,p\,\delta\,V_L^2\} + (1-m)\,p \\ &\leq m\,\alpha\,EV_L + (1-m)p. \end{aligned} \tag{2.4}$$

Hence for any p $(0 \leq p \leq 1)$

$$U(STP) - U(LTP) \geq m\,\alpha(V_S^1 - EV_L) > 0$$

and the politician chooses STP.

□

The explanation for proposition 2.1 is straightforward. Since for any fixed reelection probability private benefits are higher for STP, the politician will never opt for LTP. The next question concerns the potential for the public to make reelection probabilities conditional on the returns achieved in the first period. We use $p(V_S^1)$ and $p(0)$ to denote the reelection probabilities as a function of the possible realizations of returns in the first period. We obtain:

Proposition 2.2

Suppose that $m \leq m^*$. Then LTP is not adopted in any subgame perfect equilibrium with the conditional reelection probabilities $p(V_S^1)$ and $p(0)$.

Proof

Given reelection probabilities of whatever kind, the politician expects the following utilities:

$$U(LTP) = m\{\pi_H(\alpha V_S^1 + p(V_S^1)\,\delta\,\alpha V_L^2) + (1-\pi_H)(p(0)\,\delta\alpha V_L^2)\}$$
$$+ (1-m)\cdot\{\pi_H\,p\,(V_S^1) + (1-\pi_H)\,p(0)\}$$

$$U(STP) = m\{\alpha V_S^1\} + (1-m)\,p(V_S^1)$$

$$U(NOT) = (1-m)p(0)$$

$U(LTP) > U(STP)$ requires that $p(0) > p(V_S^1)$, because otherwise

$$U(LTP) \leq m\{\alpha \pi_H V_S^1 + \delta \alpha p(V_S^1) V_L^2\} + (1-m)\, p(V_S^1) \\ < U(STP) \tag{2.5}$$

If $p(0) > p(V_S^1)$, the politician chooses LTP instead of NOT if and only if

$$m \cdot \{\pi_H(\alpha V_S^1 + p(V_S^1)\, \delta\, \alpha\, V_L^2) + (1-\pi_H)(p\,(0)\; \delta\, \alpha\, V_L^2)\} \\ + (1-m) \cdot \{\pi_H\,(p\,(V_S^1) - p(0))\,\} \geq 0.$$

The left side is monotonically increasing in m. For $m = 0$ the left side is negative. For $m = 1$ it is positive. Hence, by the intermediate value theorem there exists a m^* such that the agent will choose LTP if and only if $m \geq m^*$.

□

Proposition 2.2 shows that if a politician is sufficiently interested in reelection, there is no choice of reelection probabilities inducing him to adopt LTP. With a high reelection probability $p(0)$, the politician will tend to choose NOT. If the public reelects candidates with $p\,(V_S^1) > p(0)$, STP yields a higher utility for the agent than LTP. Hence, the public faces the dilemma that no matter how reelection probabilities are arranged, the politician either chooses STP or NOT. Thus the reelection mechanism does not provide sufficient incentives for a politician to undertake socially efficient long-term policies as long as the policymaker himself is sufficiently interested in reelection.

It is obvious that the result in proposition 2.2 is reinforced when voters cannot commit themselves to particular reelection probabilities.

2.4 Incentive Contracts at the Reelection Stage

In this section, we consider an alternative way of inducing the politician to choose the socially efficient policy. The idea is to supplement the reelection mechanism by another incentive element. If a politician wants to be reelected, he must sign an incentive contract that makes his future utility dependent on the economic performance in the second term.

Therefore, if the politician wants to get reelected, he must accept the contract $C(\beta\, V^2)$ where β is a number $0 < \beta < 1$. If the social welfare in period 2 is realized as V^2, the reelected politician obtains a net transfer $\beta\, V^2$ if $V^2 > 0$ and must pay $-\beta\, V^2$ to the public if $V^2 < 0$. The extended stage $1\,'$ of the game now looks like this:

Stage 1$'$: The public decides on $C(\beta V^2)$ and the reelection probability function p. A politician can only stand for reelection if he accepts $C(\beta V^2)$.

For the modified game, we obtain:

Proposition 2.3
Suppose that the politician who runs for reelection must accept an incentive contract $C\,(\beta^*\, V^2)$ for some threshold level β^*. Suppose the public reelects him according to $p\,(V_S^1) = 1$ and $p\,(0) = 1$. Then the politician accepts the incentive contract $C\,(\beta^*\, V^2)$ and chooses LTP.

Proof
Because of $p(V_S^1) = p(0)$, the politician never chooses NOT. He chooses LTP if and only if

$$U(LTP) = m \cdot \{\alpha \pi_H V_S^1 + \delta \alpha V_L^2 + \delta \beta V_L^2\} + (1-m)$$
$$> U(STP) = m \cdot \{\alpha V_S^1 + \delta \beta V_S^2\} + (1-m)$$

Since $V_L^2 > 0, V_S^2 < 0$, $U(LTP) - U(STP)$ is monotonically increasing in β. Moreover, for $\beta = \alpha$, we have $U(LTP) > U(STP)$ because of our assumption $EV_L > EV_S$. Hence, there exists a threshold level β^* such that the politician chooses LTP if $\beta \geq \beta^*$ and $p(V_S^1) = p(0) = 1$. This completes the proof.

□

The bottom line of proposition 2.3 is that incentive contracts at the reelection stage can provide sufficient incentives for politicians to undertake LTP and allow the public to reelect the politician without causing policy distortions. The requirement of accepting the incentive contract acts as an entry barrier to reelection. The entry barrier will deter a politician from seeking reelection if he has not invested in long-term policies.

At this stage, we must deal with the question of who determines the content of the incentive contract. There are three possibilities. First, the contract could be determined by a court, be it the constitutional court or a special court. Second, the incentive contract could be determined by polls collecting the opinions of voters and thus by the public. It is obvious that the public would propose $C(\beta^* V^2)$ if the discounted transfer $\delta\beta V_L^2$ to the politician is smaller than the additional utility obtained by LTP. Thus,

Corollary 2.1
Voters propose $C(\beta^* V^2)$ *in period 1 if* $EV_L - EV_N > \delta\beta^* V_L^2$.

In general, one might expect the transfer to the politician to be much smaller than the welfare gains from good policies. If not, the distortion by not adopting LTP may not be significant and thus there may be no real problem. Third, we could allow the politician to offer the incentive contract he would like to have. We immediately obtain:

Corollary 2.2
Suppose that

$$\overline{\beta} = \frac{EV_L - EV_N}{V_L^2} > \beta^* \tag{2.6}$$

Then there exists a unique subgame perfect equilibrium in which the politician offers $C(\overline{\beta}V^2)$ *and the public commits itself to* $p\,(V_S^1) = 1$ *and* $p\,(0) = 1$.

The corollary follows directly from the preceding discussion. The politician can gain more by offering $C(\overline{\beta}V^2)$ and choosing LTP than with any other combination of investment decision and incentive contract. The politician extracts all the surplus by demanding the welfare difference between the welfare of LTP and the next-best alternative.

Note, however, that this only works if the public commits itself to reelection before the politician has decided on his policies. Otherwise, the public would tend to renege on its reelection promise. If the politician has adopted LTP and has offered $C(\overline{\beta}V^2)$, it is better for the public not to reelect the politician in order to save $\overline{\beta}V^2$.

To sum up, leaving the determination of incentive contracts to politicians introduces two problems. First, the politician takes too much for himself if the public commits itself to a reelection scheme after having observed the incentive contract of the politician but before investment decisions have been made. If the public does not or cannot commit itself, any incentive contract which involves transfers from the public to politicians would lead to zero reelection and thus to STP. One solution to this problem is to make the incentive contract for a politician binding as soon as he stands for reelection, regardless of whether he will remain in office. Such "golden parachute" clauses in incentive contracts could solve the time-inconsistency problem inherent in the voters' reelection decision.

But there is still the problem that politicians may try to demand excessive transfers once elected. This problem can be solved by offering contracts before the first election takes place. At that stage at least two politicians will compete and standard Bertrand reasoning would imply that $C(\beta^* V^2)$ will be offered by both politicians competing for office. The next chapter contains a detailed analysis in the context of observable policies of whether competing politicians offer socially desirable incentive contracts.

2.5 Other Sources of Inefficiencies

In this section we suggest that the combination of incentive contracts and elections can be used to obviate inefficient policy decisions stemming from sources we have not considered yet. With appropriate modifications, incentive contracts might be used to alleviate the inefficiency of democracies identified in the work of Besley and Coate (1998) and in specific contexts by Glazer (1989) and Gersbach (1993) caused by the inability of current voters to commit future citizens to adhere to particular policies.[5]

A closely related argument suggests that governments run inefficiently large deficits (Persson and Svensson (1989), Alesina and Tabellini (1990) and Tabellini and Alesina (1990)). The party in power may choose to run a deficit in the current period. This serves to constrain the choices of those in power in the future. Here again, the dual mechanism of incentive contracts and elections could alleviate the inefficiency in line with the arguments advanced in this chapter.

2.6 Practical Issues

Our simple analysis suggests that the dual mechanism of competition for elections and incentive contracts might alleviate some of the inefficiencies in democratic decision-making. However, there are a number of practical issues. For instance which quantitative measures should be used for the incentive contract. This is fairly obvious in the case of European unemployment, because the incentive contract can be based on the average unemployment rate. But a definition problem remains since the unemployment rate is defined in many different ways. Hence, there is a need to agree upon a definition that cannot be changed and manipulated once it has been adopted.

Moreover, it is hard to measure social welfare beyond macroeconomic indicators and very often politicians are judged by other

[5] Similarly, the inefficiency caused by voters' myopia as described by Cohen and Noll (1990) and Buchanan and Wagner (1977) can be mitigated by incentive contracts.

factors. For instance, voters may support a candidate based on personal qualities such as leadership or communication skills. A prominent example is the victory of George W. Bush in the presidential election in the USA in 2000, since all economic indicators were looking highly favorable for Democrats. Clearly, such issues as leadership or communication skills are not contractible.

These serious difficulties notwithstanding, one could try to use incentive contracts in a limited way. Politicians in the executive and legislative branch are typically concerned with many different issues. Whereas issues such as unemployment or crime can be quantified with sufficient precision, this is not the case for other issues such as reforming health care or the judicial system. Therefore, performance in a significant part of their activities cannot be measured with any real degree of precision. As we know from the theory of multi-task incentive problems, outlined in Holmström and Milgrom (1991), severe measurement constraints can make it impossible to use task-specific performance schemes or aggregate performance measures. For instance, if politicians are only judged by their employment performance, they may simply inflate the public sector to meet the required standard and neglect other important issues.

Nevertheless, the multi-task and the measurement problem might be alleviated by the dual mechanism proposed in this chapter. A politician can only stand for reelection if he is willing to base his future income or the right for future reelection on the performance on one issue, say unemployment. If he accepts the incentive component, he can stand for reelection and voters can judge his performance on the remaining issues. If he has accepted the incentive contract, but only worked to reduce unemployment, voters may not reelect him because he has a bad record on other important issues. Therefore, the hierarchical incentive scheme can cause the politician to choose the socially desirable policy for one dimension without neglecting other issues. See Gersbach and Liessem (2003) for a formal analysis of this argument.[6] Moreover, new informational intermediaries may develop for the political sphere which improve the scope to make campaign promises binding through contracts.

Still, many pressing issues during a term of a politician may not be known or sufficiently known when the politician takes over the office. For instance, one could argue that the most pressing issue that George Bush senior faced in his term as president of the USA was the Iraq's invasion of Kuwait. Since this issue was not known in its pressing and threatening way it would have been difficult or impossible to write an incentive contract on the resolution of the war at the beginning of Bush's presidency. In summary, there are a number of practical and conceptual issues for the combination of elections and incentive contracts.

2.7 Conclusion

In this chapter, we have suggested a simple solution to the problem that politicians may not be sufficiently motivated to undertake long-term socially beneficial policies, when the public is not able to effectively distinguish between the types of policies. In the next chapter we consider an alternative set-up where policy

[6] Another interesting application of incentive contracts and elections might be underinvestment problems arising from distributive politics within a majoritarian institution explored by Leblanc, Snyder, and Tripathi (2000), building on the bargaining model of Baron and Ferejohn (1989).

and their consequences are known to voters. Complications arise because we allow that politicians can offer themselves incentive contracts during campaigns and voters may have limited information regarding the type of the politician.

3. Short-Termism and Competition for Incentive Contracts[1]

3.1 Introduction

In the last chapter we have illustrated that democratic elections cannot motivate politicians to undertake long-term socially beneficial projects when politicians are short-term oriented or future elections do not sufficiently reflect the success of past policies. In this chapter we suggest that competition between politicians for incentive contracts and elections can motivate them to undertake socially desirable long-term projects while at the same time preserving the democratic legitimation of politicians.

The essential differences to the last chapter are threefold. First, we assume that voters observe the policies undertaken before reelection takes place and thus the reelection mechanism has more bite. Second, we allow that politicians can offer incentive contracts themselves during political campaigns. Third, the public may face asymmetric information regarding the type of politician.

We consider a model where two candidates compete for office in an initial election period and for subsequent reelection. Candidates are motivated by the offices they hold and by the policies they undertake. Once a candidate is elected he can under-

[1] A previous version of the analysis developed in this chapter has appeared in Gersbach (2004a).

take socially desirable long-term projects, opt for inefficient short-term projects or stick to the status quo. Returns from long-term projects only accrue to voters in a second election period. The problem for the public is that the discount factor of the politician may be not sufficiently high and/or reelection prospects are uncertain and only loosely connected to policy results. In such cases, politicians behave short-term oriented and the public cannot sufficiently motivate a politician to invest in long-term projects. This holds even if the public could commit itself to reelection.

To alleviate these inefficiencies we suggest the electorate use a hierarchy of incentive contracts and elections. Candidates are given the possibility of offering incentive contracts when campaigning for office for the first election period. The incentive contract stipulates that in the event of reelection the politician's utility or income in the second election period depends on policy returns such as the level of unemployment. Incentive contracts become binding as soon as the politician decides to stand for reelection and is actually reelected. Candidates are free to offer empty contracts or contracts making their income depend on long-term returns.

Our findings are as follows: First, if the discount factor is below a certain threshold, the public cannot motivate the politician to undertake long-term projects by election alone. This also holds even if the public commits itself to a reelection scheme. If reelection prospects are sufficiently uncertain, politicians may not be motivated to undertake long-term policies even if they do not discount the future at all.

Second, when politicians can offer incentive contracts and the public commits itself to a reelection scheme, the result is a unique equilibrium. Both politicians offer the same contract. The equilibrium contract stipulates future transfers ensuring that the politician with the lower discount factor will be indifferent about choosing the long-term project or the short-term project. Transfers are interpreted in a wide sense. For instance, a politician may receive special monetary remunerations in the future or he may become a special honorary citizen if his policies generate long-term benefits for society. The politician with the larger discount factor is elected; his reelection is certain and he will take the socially efficient long-term decision.

In the following, we relax two of the assumptions upon which the previous findings have built. Our third result shows that the hierarchy of elections and incentive contracts will still induce politicians to undertake socially beneficial long-term projects even if the public cannot commit itself to any future reelection behavior. We consider two reasons why current voters may not be able to commit themselves to a certain future voting behavior: the democratic requirement for unconstrained voting in every election and incentives to reject the incumbent in order to economize on his future remunerations.[2] In the first case, future transfers to an elected politician undertaking the long-term project must be higher in equilibrium. In the second case, incentive contracts must include a golden parachute clause guaranteeing a future bonus to a politician even he is no longer in office.

In our fourth result we allow for the case where the public does not know the discount factors of politicians competing for office. In the corresponding game between politicians and the public under asymmetric information, there exists a Bayesian Nash equi-

[2] The second reason is less important since the remuneration of a politician creates only a negligible burden per capita for the public.

librium in which all types of politicians will undertake beneficial long-term projects. Under uncertainty about the politician's discount factor, the public will have to grant benefits to the politician corresponding to the benefits under certainty with the lowest possible realization of the discount factor.

To sum up, competition among politicians for the hierarchy of incentive contracts and elections appears to be a reasonably robust mechanism to overcome short-termism. Since the contracts suggested in this chapter have no counterpart in reality there are a number of practical issues regarding the application of the hierarchy of incentive contracts and elections which we will address in the final section.

This chapter is related to the literature about electoral accountability which was initiated by Barro (1973) and Ferejohn (1986) and recently extended by Persson, Roland, and Tabellini (1997) (see Persson and Tabellini (2000) for surveys). Politicians and voters are assumed to have divergent interests, and elections are a means by which voters control the misbehavior of politicians, since the possibility of reelection induces self-interested politicians to act on behalf of the interests of the electorate. In this chapter, we introduce competition of politicians for incentive contracts and elections as a novel element in politics. We combine contractual and electoral accountability while at the same time preserving the democratic legitimation of politicians.

In this chapter we introduce competition of politicians for incentive contracts and elections in democracies with periodic, free and anonymous elections. For simplicity, we consider a model where politicians and voters differ with respect to their relative valuation of future and current utilities. This is a tractable model for the analysis of how competition for incentive contracts and elections may alleviate inefficiencies in democracies. In practice, as is discussed in the concluding section, democracies may produce inefficiencies for a wide variety of reasons and it is not clear whether the source of inefficiency we are focusing on is the most important one. However, the ideas presented in this chapter may be useful when applied to other kinds of inefficiencies in political processes.

The chapter is organized as follows: In the next section, we outline the model and our assumptions. In section 3, we consider the potentialities and limitations of the election mechanism for achieving optimal decisions. In section 4, we show that competition among politicians for incentive contracts and election induces socially optimal decisions. In section 5, we extend our analysis to the non-commitment case. In section 6, we discuss asymmetric information. Section 7 presents our conclusions.

3.2 The Model

The game we are analyzing is a dynamic game with two periods. The model has a similar flavor as in the last chapter, but now we assume that voters can observe the policies adopted by an elected candidate. We assume that the politician (or agent) is risk-neutral. Returns from projects are denoted by V and will be indexed according to the type of project and the period involved. The game is given as follows:

Stage 1: At the beginning of period 1 two politicians, denoted by $i = 1, 2$, offer incentive contracts $C_1(\beta_1 V^2)$ and $C_2(\beta_2 V^2)$ with the following interpretation: if politician i is reelected in period 2, he receives a net transfer $\beta_i V^2$ if $V^2 > 0$ and has to pay $\beta_i V^2$ if $V^2 < 0$, where $0 \leq \beta_i \leq 1$.

Stage 2: The public decides whether the politician is elected. We use p_i $(0 \leq p_i \leq 1)$ to denote the probability that politician i will be elected $(p_1 + p_2 = 1)$.

Stage 3: The agent must decide whether to undertake certain projects. He has three options. He can undertake a short-term policy (STP) generating a positive return $V_S^1 > 0$ in this period, but a negative return $V_S^2 < 0$ next period. The second option is a long-term policy (LTP). For simplicity of presentation the long-term policy is assumed to have no short-term consequences, i.e. $V_L^1 = 0$. LTP generates positive payoffs $V_L^2 > 0$ in the next period. The last option for the policy-maker is to continue with the status quo and to do nothing (NOT). Payoffs in this case are normalized to zero in both periods: $V_N^1 = V_N^2 = 0$.

To sum up, the elected politician decides among his options in $\{STP, LTP, NOT\}$.

Stage 4: The returns from the first period are apparent. The elected politician decides whether he wants to run for office again. The public decides on the reelection of the politician. The probability that politician i is reelected is denoted by q_i, $(0 \leq q_i \leq 1,\ q_1 + q_2 = 1)$. Reelected politicians obtain or pay the transfers stipulated in the incentive contract.

All costs and benefits are measured in dollars. There are many examples of LTP projects versus STP or NOT projects as we have discussed in the last chapter.

We assume that contracts can be conditioned on social returns measured for instance by GDP growth or criminal statistics.[3] However, we assume that contracts cannot be conditioned on the policy choice itself. The latter assumption follows the reasoning in the incomplete contract literature (see the survey of Hart (1995)). In politics complete contracts would require to write all conceivable laws into contracts before they are initiated in Parliament which appears to be impossible.

We assume that a politician can generate private returns as long as he is in power. If he is in power and realizes a social project return V in a given period, we assume that his private benefits are:

$$R_i = \alpha V \tag{3.1}$$

where α is some number $0 < \alpha < 1$.[4] The above assumption can be justified by an interest group story (see e.g. Mueller (1989)). Alternatively, the politician is genuinely concerned about the social returns he generates as long as the outcomes of policies occur while he is in office. We follow the latter interpretation, which simplifies the analysis.[5]

---

[3] For simplicity of exposition contracts are assumed to be linear in social returns. Since returns in the second period can only take three values, this assumption could easily be relaxed.

[4] An alternative assumption about private returns would be $R_i = \max[\alpha V, 0]$ as in the last chapter. This assumption would strengthen the need to use incentive contracts because STP becomes more attractive.

[5] The first interpretation yields the same qualitative conclusions, but the public needs to take into account that some returns from projects are channeled to the politician or the interest group supporting him.

We concentrate on the agent's utility in period 1 when politicians stand for election for the first time. We assume that the utility of an agent increases both in the private benefits from holding office, denoted by $B > 0$, and from the private benefits of investment projects. In particular, we assume

$$U_i = p_i \left((1-m)B + m\, R_i^1 + \delta_i q_i \left((1-m)B + m(R_i^2 + \beta_i V^2)\right)\right)$$

where $R_i^1 = \alpha V^1$ and $R_i^2 = \alpha V^2$ are the private returns in period 1 and 2, respectively. δ_i is the discount factor of politician i, $(0 \leq \delta_i \leq 1)$. The parameter m, with $0 < m < 1$, which is assumed to be the same for both politicians, is the significance the agent assigns to private returns from projects and $1-m$ is the significance of benefits from holding office. A weight m close to 1 means that the agent is mainly motivated by the policies he implements. A low value for m corresponds to an agent being mainly concerned to hold office. The utility of outside options is normalized to zero. Throughout the chapter we assume that $(1-m)B$ is sufficiently large such that net utilities of politicians in the second period are always non-negative.

To simplify the exposition we use

- $U_i^L(\beta_i, RE)$ to denote the utility of an elected politician i if he has offered the contract $C_i(\beta_i V^2)$, undertakes LTP and is reelected:

$$\begin{aligned} U_i^L(\beta_i, RE) = &(1-m)B \\ &+ \delta_i \left\{(1-m)B + mV_L^2(\alpha + \beta_i)\right\} \end{aligned} \tag{3.2}$$

- $U_i^S(\beta_i, RE)$ to denote the utility of an elected politician i if he has offered $C_i(\beta_i V^2)$, undertakes STP and is reelected:

$$U_i^S(\beta_i, RE) = (1-m)B + m\alpha V_S^1 + \delta_i\{(1-m)B + mV_S^2(\alpha+\beta_i)\} \tag{3.3}$$

- $U_i^S(NRE)$ to denote the utility of an elected politician i if he has offered $C_i(\beta_i V^2)$, undertakes STP and does not stand for reelection:

$$U_i^S(NRE) = (1-m)B + m\alpha V_S^1 \tag{3.4}$$

We allow for the fact that politicians may differ in their discount factor δ_i ($i = 1, 2$) with $0 \leq \delta_i \leq 1$. In many cases such differences are known to the public. Consider for example the election race between the incumbent, Kohl, and the challenger, Schröder, in 1998 in Germany. It was well-known that Kohl was competing for a final term whereas Schröder wanted to start his era as chancellor. Therefore, we assume in the following that δ_1 and δ_2 are known to the public and we label candidates such that $\delta_1 \leq \delta_2$. Later we will relax the informational assumptions about discount factors.

We denote the expected returns to the public from the options STP, LTP and NOT by EV_S, EV_L, and EV_N, respectively. Thus:

$$EV_S = V_S^1 + \bar{\delta}\, V_S^2$$
$$EV_L = \bar{\delta}\, V_L^2$$
$$EV_N = V_N^1 + \bar{\delta}\, V_N^2 = 0$$

$\bar{\delta}$ is the discount factor of the public ($0 < \bar{\delta} \leq 1$). The social discount factor may be higher or lower than that of the politicians. We assume that

$$EV_L > EV_N > EV_S$$
$$V_S^1 > EV_L$$

The preceding assumption immediately implies that in social terms the optimal policy is LTP. To simplify the presentation, we employ three tie-breaking rules. First, if two politicians generate the same social welfare, the public will elect the politician with the higher discount factor. Second, if both politicians are equally good in terms of social welfare and are identical in terms of the discount factor, both politicians have the same chance $p_1 = p_2 = \frac{1}{2}$ of being elected. Third, if a politician is indifferent as to two types of policies, he will select the one that yields higher social welfare. These tie-breaking rules simplify the exposition but are not essential for the results.

3.3 Elections

In this section we discuss how the public can motivate politicians to undertake *LTP* if the only instrument available is the election mechanism. We assume that the public can commit itself in stage 1 to its reelection scheme in stage 4 with the two reelection probabilities $q(V_S^1)$ at STP and $q(0)$ at LTP. This gives the best chance of elections inducing elected politicians to choose *LTP*. However, no incentive contracts can be offered. Then, we obtain:

Proposition 3.1

Suppose the public can commit to a reelection scheme and that $\delta_i \leq \delta(m)$ *with*

$$\delta(m) = \frac{m\alpha V_S^1}{(1-m)B + m\alpha V_L^2} \tag{3.5}$$

Then, the politician cannot be motivated by elections alone to adopt LTP.

Proof

It is obvious that the politician will never choose NOT under any reelection scheme, because he benefits equally or more from LTP or STP. Additionally, it is obvious that the optimal reelection scheme for voters is $q(0) = 1$ and $q(V_S^1) = 0$, which is the maximum spread to deter the politician from choosing STP. The critical discount factor is then determined by setting $U_i^L(0, RE) = U_i^S(NRE)$ which yields:

$$\delta(m) = \frac{m\alpha V_S^1}{(1-m)B + m\alpha V_L^2} \tag{3.6}$$

If $\delta(m) < 1$ a politician with $\delta_i \in [\delta(m), 1]$ will choose LTP under the reelection scheme $q(0) = 1$ and $q(V_S^1) = 0$ and STP otherwise.

□

We immediately obtain $\delta(0) = 0$ and

$$\frac{\partial \delta(m)}{\partial m} = \frac{\alpha V_S^1 B}{\{(1-m)B + m\alpha V_L^2\}^2} > 0 \tag{3.7}$$

Therefore, since $m > 0$, we have a range for the discount factor at which politicians will not choose the socially efficient policy. Note that voters are assumed to be fully rational and infer negative future returns from the positive returns of short-term projects in the first election period.

The underinvestment problem becomes more pronounced when the public cannot commit to a reelection scheme, which is the natural assumption for democratic decision-making. As an example for the severity of the underinvestment problem in such cases, suppose that the public votes prospectively and that past policy performance does not influence reelection chances.[6] In particular, suppose that $q(0) = q(V_S^1) = \frac{1}{2}$ and thus, from the perspective of the beginning of the first term the incumbent is reelected with probability one half and thus independently of the adopted policy. Then we obtain:

Proposition 3.2

Suppose that the public cannot commit to a reelection scheme. Suppose $q(0) = q(V_S^1) = \frac{1}{2}$ and that $\delta_i \leq \hat{\delta}(m)$ with:

$$\hat{\delta}(m) = \max\left\{\frac{2m\,\alpha\,V_S^1}{(1-m)\,B + m\,\alpha\,V_L^2}, \frac{2V_S^1}{V_L^2 - V_S^2}\right\}$$

Then, the politician cannot be motivated by elections to undertake LTP.

Proof

The proof is similar to proposition 3.1. Now we have to compare $U_i^L(0, RE)$ with $U_i^S(0, RE)$ and $U_i^S(NRE)$. The utilities $U_i^L(0, RE)$ and $U_i^S(0, RE)$ are now calculated by using the reelection probability $\frac{1}{2}$. Since incentive contracts are not available, we set $\beta = 0$ and keep the notation introduced in section 3.2. The comparisons yield:

$$\delta_i = \frac{2V_S^1}{V_L^2 - V_S^2}$$

$$\delta_i = \frac{2m\,\alpha\,V_S^1}{(1-m)B + m\,\alpha\,V_L^2}$$

which establishes the proposition.

□

[6] This is an extreme assumption and solely made for expositional purposes.

The preceding proposition illustrates that the underinvestment problem is severe if reelection prospects are not (or only loosely) connected with policies undertaken in the past. In such cases, as the following corollary illustrates, there are circumstances when no politician invests in LTP, independently of his discount factor.

Corollary 3.1

Suppose that the public cannot commit to a reelection scheme. Suppose that $q(0) = q(V_S^1) = \frac{1}{2}$ *and* $V_S^1 + \frac{1}{2}V_S^2 > \frac{1}{2}V_L^2$. *Then, no politician can be motivated by elections to adopt* LTP.

The corollary immediately follows from proposition 3.2. Under $V_S^1 + \frac{1}{2}V_S^2 > \frac{1}{2}V_L^2$ the critical discount factor becomes larger than 1 and thus politicians will choose STP. Intuitively, if the short-term project is not too bad, the low probability of reelection induces politicians to adopt the STP since they can benefit with certainty from returns in the first term and they have no influence on their reelection chances. Note that the weight m on policy in the objective function of the politician is irrelevant in corollary 3.1 since the politician expects the same utility from holding office per se under LTP and STP. In the next section we begin to address how incentive contracts can overcome the inefficiencies identified in this section.

3.4 Competition for the Incentive Contracts

In this section we consider the whole game and allow politicians to offer incentive contracts before the first election takes place. We first assume in this section that voters can commit themselves to a reelection scheme in stage 1, in order to compare the competition for incentive contracts and elections with the previous section. We obtain:

Proposition 3.3

Suppose $0 < \delta_1 < \delta_2 \leq \delta(m)$. *There then exists a unique subgame perfect equilibrium*

$$\Big\{ C_1(\beta_1 V^2), C_2(\beta_2 V^2), p_1 = 0, p_2 = 1, \\ q_1(0) = 1, q_2(0) = 1, q_1(V_S^1) = 0, q_2(V_S^1) = 0 \Big\}$$

with

$$\beta_1 = \beta_2 = \overline{\beta} = \frac{m\alpha V_S^1 - \delta_1 \left\{(1-m)B + m\alpha V_L^2\right\}}{m\delta_1 V_L^2} \tag{3.8}$$

if

$$\overline{\delta}\overline{\beta}V_L^2 < EV_L - EV_S \tag{3.9}$$

The proof is given in the appendix.

Proposition 3.3 shows that the hierarchy of elections and incentive contracts eliminates inefficient decision-making in politics at the cost of future transfers to the elected politician. Both politicians offer the same contract. The equilibrium contract stipulates future transfers ensuring that the politician with the lower discount factor will be indifferent about choosing the long-term project or the short-term project. The politician with the larger discount factor is elected; his prospects of reelection are certain and he will take the socially efficient long-term decision.

In the following, we relax the assumptions upon which the result has built. In proposition 3.3 voters are assumed to commit themselves to a state-dependent reelection scheme. Competition for incentive contracts and election can still work if the public can only commit itself to a fixed reelection probability, as is illustrated in the next corollary.

Corollary 3.2

Suppose the public could only commit itself to a fixed reelection probability. Then the equilibrium with $\overline{\beta}$ in proposition 3.3 still holds correspondingly with $q_1 = q_2 = 1$ if

$$(1-m)B + mV_S^2(\alpha + \overline{\beta}) < 0 \tag{3.10}$$

The proof is analogous to the proof of proposition 3.3 because (3.10) directly implies $U_i^S(NRE) > U_i^S(\overline{\beta}, RE)$ and therefore, with incentive contracts $C(\overline{\beta}V^2)$, neither politician has an incentive to adopt STP and to stand for reelection. To examine the case of non-commitment in the next section, we denote the equilibrium value for β by $\overline{\beta}^C$. Note that $\overline{\beta}^C$ in equation (3.8) depends negatively on δ_1. A large δ_1 decreases the costs of transfers to the politician and harms the elected politician 2. With appropriate modifications in the proof, proposition 3.3 can be extended to the case when politicians are identical:

Corollary 3.3

Suppose $\delta_1 = \delta_2 \leq \delta(m)$. There then exists a unique subgame perfect equilibrium

$$\Big\{ C_1(\beta_1 V^2), C_2(\beta_2 V^2), p_1 = \frac{1}{2}, p_2 = \frac{1}{2},$$

$$q_1(0) = 1, q_2(0) = 1, q_1(V_S^1) = 0, q_2(V_S^1) = 0 \Big\}$$

with

$$\beta_1 = \beta_2 = \overline{\beta}^C = \frac{m\alpha V_S^1 - \delta_1 \left\{(1-m)B + m\alpha V_L^2\right\}}{m\delta_1 V_L^2} \tag{3.11}$$

if

$$\bar{\delta}\beta^C V_L^2 < EV_L - EV_S \tag{3.12}$$

3.5 Competition Without Commitment

The assumption that voters can commit themselves to a reelection scheme has mainly been made in order to give the election mechanism the best chance to motivate political leaders to invest in long-term, efficient projects. However, from a strictly democratic point of view, voters are unable to commit future citizens to adhere to a particular voting behavior. The contracting problem is rooted in the uncertainty about future electoral interests and the liberal principle of democracies to allow for free and anonymous voting behavior in elections.

The impossibility of commitment to future voting behavior represents another source of inefficiency outlined in the previous chapter. We can integrate the impossibility of commitment into our model. There are two non-commitment problems: incentives of voters to reject an incumbent so as to economize on his future remunerations and the democratic requirement for unconstrained voting in every election. We deal with the latter case first. Suppose there is complete uncertainty about the voting behavior of future generations such that an elected politician today has an *a priori* expectation of reelection of $q_i = \frac{1}{2}$ independently of his actions in the past.[7] This is an opposite pole to the commitment case where q_i is either 1 if the choice of LTP is expected or 0 otherwise. Though we think that intermediate cases are the most plausible, it is instructive to compare these polar opposites. For the non-commitment case we obtain:

[7] See also the retrospective voting approach (Ferejohn (1986)).

Proposition 3.4

Suppose $\delta_1 \leq \delta_2 \leq \delta(m)$*. There then exists a unique subgame perfect equilibrium*

$$\left\{C_1(\beta_1 V^2), C_2(\beta_2 V^2), p_1 = 0, p_2 = 1, \right.$$
$$\left. q_1(0) = \frac{1}{2}, q_2(0) = \frac{1}{2}, q_1(V_S^1) = \frac{1}{2}, q_2(V_S^1) = \frac{1}{2}\right\}$$

with

$$\beta_1 = \beta_2 = \overline{\beta}^{NC} = \tag{3.13}$$

$$\max\left\{\frac{2m\alpha V_S^1 - \delta_1\left\{(1-m)B + m\alpha V_L^2\right\}}{m\delta_1 V_L^2}, \frac{2\alpha V_S^1 - \delta_1\alpha(V_L^2 - V_S^2)}{\delta_1(V_L^2 - V_S^2)}\right\}$$

if [8]

$$\overline{\delta}\,\overline{\beta}^{NC} V_L^2 < EV_L - EV_S \tag{3.14}$$

The proof is similar to the commitment case. But now we have to compare $U_i^L(\overline{\beta}, RE)$ with $U_i^S(\overline{\beta}, RE)$ and $U_i^S(NRE)$, and the utility in the second period must be evaluated with $q_1 = q_2 = \frac{1}{2}$ instead of certain reelection. An immediate consequence is

Corollary 3.4

$$\overline{\beta}^{NC} > \overline{\beta}^{C} \tag{3.15}$$

It is obvious that under non-commitment it requires a higher future transfer to make the politician with the lower discount factor indifferent as to LTP and STP. The impossibility of the present generation of voters to commit future voters to a particular election choice entails the larger transfer a reelected politician must receive if he undertakes LTP.

[8] Condition (3.14) is sufficient but since politicians selecting STP have a chance to be reelected the proposition also holds on weaker conditions.

There might be a second and even more extreme case of non-commitment if voters at the reelection date definitely reject the incumbent, in order to economize on future remunerations for the politician. In this case the nature of the incentive contracts can be amended in the following way. The incentive contract becomes effective if the politician stands for reelection, independently of whether he is reelected. Thus, he can receive future benefits from LTP even if he is not in office anymore. We call such incentive contracts golden parachute contracts; they are denoted by C^{Pa}. The utility for a politician if he is not reelected is denoted by $U_i^{para}(\beta_i, V^2, NRE)$ and given by

$$U_i^{para}(\beta_i, V^2, NRE) = p_i \left((1-m)B + mR_i^1 + \delta_i \beta_i V^2\right) \quad (3.16)$$

We immediately obtain:

Proposition 3.5

Suppose that $\delta_1 < \delta_2 < \delta(m)$ and politicians can offer golden parachute contracts and the politician elected in period 1 is rejected with certainty. There then exists a unique subgame perfect equilibrium where politicians offer golden parachute contracts.

$$\left\{C_1^{Pa}(\beta_1 V^2), C_2^{Pa}(\beta_2 V^2), p_1 = 0, p_2 = 1\right\} \quad (3.17)$$

with

$$\beta_1 = \beta_2 = \overline{\beta}^{NCPa} = \frac{\alpha V_S^1}{\delta_1 V_L^2} \quad (3.18)$$

if

$$\bar{\delta}\bar{\beta}^{NCPa} V_L^2 < EV_L - EV_S \quad (3.19)$$

The proof is analogous to the previous proposition. Note that $\overline{\beta}^{NCPa}$ is determined by $U_1^{para}(\bar{\beta}^{NCPa}, V_L^2, NRE) = U_1^S(NRE)$ because a politician is not forced to offer a parachute contract. While we have assumed an extreme case of non-commitment in proposition 3.5, it is obvious that the option to offer golden parachute contracts also works for intermediate values of reelection probability when standard contracts cannot induce LTP with lower costs for the public.

3.6 Asymmetric Information

While politicians' discount factors may be well-known in some circumstances, there may be more uncertainty in other cases. For instance, when two politicians are competing for office for the first time, the public may be uncertain about the preferences of the politicians and in particular about discount factors. To explore how asymmetric information affects the functioning of the dual mechanism - incentive contracts and elections - we assume that the public knows that both politicians competing for office have discount factors δ^H with probability w and $\delta^L < \delta^H$ with probability $1 - w$. We assume that politicians know the discount factor of their opponent.[9] We further use b_i $(i = 1, 2)$ to denote the beliefs of the public that politician i has discount factor δ^H when incentive contracts $C_1(\beta_1 V^2)$ and $C_2(\beta_2 V^2)$ have been offered. Then we look for perfect Bayesian equilibria of the election and the incentive contract game. As an example when the public can commit to a reelection scheme we obtain:

Proposition 3.6

There exists a perfect Bayesian Nash equilibrium[10]

$$\{C_1(\beta_1^* V^2), C_2(\beta_2^* V^2), p_1^*, p_2^*, q_1^*(0), q_2^*(0), q_1^*(V_S^1), q_2^*(V_S^1), b_1^*, b_2^*\}$$

---

9 The assumption appears to be plausible because of the superior knowledge politicians have about each other through their daily interaction.

10 Other equilibria exist. For instance, lower values of $\overline{\beta}^{AI}$ can be supported as equilibria as well. Moreover, one can apply refinements to the Bayesian equilibrium notion to support particular values of β_1 and β_2 in equilibrium. Details are available upon request.

$$if\ \overline{\delta} \cdot \overline{\beta}^{AI} V_L^2 < EV_L - EV_S \tag{3.20}$$

with

(i)

$$\beta_1^* = \beta_2^* = \overline{\beta}^{AI} = \frac{m\alpha V_S^1 - \delta^L \{(1-m)B + m\alpha V_L^2\}}{m\delta^L V_L^2} \tag{3.21}$$

(ii) An elected politician chooses LTP in equilibrium.

(iii)

$$b_1^*(\beta_1, \beta_2) = \begin{cases} w \text{ if } \beta_1 = \overline{\beta}^{AI} \\ 0 \text{ otherwise} \end{cases} \tag{3.22}$$

$$b_2^*(\beta_1, \beta_2) = \begin{cases} w \text{ if } \beta_2 = \overline{\beta}^{AI} \\ 0 \text{ otherwise} \end{cases} \tag{3.23}$$

(iv)

$$p_1^*(\beta_1, \beta_2) = \begin{cases} \frac{1}{2} \text{ if } \beta_1 = \beta_2 \\ \frac{1}{2} \text{ if } \overline{\beta}^{AI} > \beta_1 > \beta_2 \text{ or } \overline{\beta}^{AI} > \beta_2 > \beta_1 \\ 1 \text{ if } \beta_1 = \overline{\beta}^{AI} \quad \text{and } \beta_2 \neq \overline{\beta}^{AI} \\ 1 \text{ if } \beta_1 > \overline{\beta}^{AI} > \beta_2 \text{ or } \overline{\beta}^{AI} < \beta_1 < \beta_2 \\ 0 \quad \text{otherwise} \end{cases} \tag{3.24}$$

$$p_2^*(\beta_1, \beta_2) = \begin{cases} \frac{1}{2} \text{ if } \beta_1 = \beta_2 \\ \frac{1}{2} \text{ if } \overline{\beta}^{AI} > \beta_1 > \beta_2 \text{ or } \overline{\beta}^{AI} > \beta_2 > \beta_1 \\ 1 \text{ if } \beta_2 = \overline{\beta}^{AI} \quad \text{and } \beta_1 \neq \overline{\beta}^{AI} \\ 1 \text{ if } \beta_2 > \overline{\beta}^{AI} > \beta_1 \text{ or } \overline{\beta}^{AI} < \beta_2 < \beta_1 \\ 0 \quad \text{otherwise} \end{cases} \tag{3.25}$$

(v)

$$\begin{aligned} q_1^*(0) \quad &= q_2^*(0) \quad = 1 \\ q_1^*(V_S^1) &= q_2^*(V_S^1) = 0 \end{aligned} \tag{3.26}$$

The proof is given in Gersbach (2004a).

Proposition 3.6 shows that the hierarchy of incentive contracts and elections also works under incomplete information. But $\overline{\beta}^{AI}$ is evaluated at the lower discount factor and thus the public is forced to accept transfers to the politician higher than those expected when the public knew δ to be either δ^L or δ^H in advance.

3.7 Conclusion

Our simple analysis suggests that the dual mechanism of competition for elections and incentive contracts might alleviate some of the inefficiencies in democratic decision-making. However, there are many practical issues to be taken care of as discussed in the last chapter.

Moreover, the literature has identified a number of further important inefficiencies in the political system. How the dual mechanism can be applied for these kinds of inefficiencies and for more sophisticated models might be a useful extension. An even more challenging task would be the use of incentive contracts when policies are determined through a combination of decisions at the federal and the local level. Whether supplementing a two-tier government by incentive contracts at the federal or local level would lead to more efficient provision of public goods is an open question.

While the actual reach of the dual mechanism can only be judged after these avenues have been explored and a number of obvious practical issues have been addressed, this and the last chapter have illustrated that well-designed incentive elements might complement the reelection mechanism in motivating politicians to invest in socially desirable long-term policies.

3.8 Appendix

Proof of proposition 3.3

The condition ensures that the public is better off committing itself to reelection and accepting a politician with $C_1(\overline{\beta}V^2)$ than setting $q_1(0) = q_2(0) = 0$ which avoids the transfer $\overline{\beta}V_L^2$ but implies STP. The public sets $q_i(V_S^1) = 0$ because they will receive negative returns in period 2, when a politician undertakes STP. Thus $U_i^S(NRE) = U_i^S(\beta_i, RE)$. $\overline{\beta}$ is constructed such that the first candidate is indifferent as to STP and LTP if elected. Hence $\overline{\beta}$ is determined by

$$U_1^L(\overline{\beta}, RE) = U_1^S(NRE) \quad (3.27)$$

which gives equation (3.8). Since the incentive contract is irrelevant if a candidate does not want to stand for reelection we have:

$$U_1^S(NRE) = U_2^S(NRE). \quad (3.28)$$

Because of $\delta_1 < \delta_2$ we have:

$$U_2^L(\overline{\beta}, RE) > U_1^L(\overline{\beta}, RE). \quad (3.29)$$

Candidate 2 has a strict preference for LTP if elected, in contrast to the indifference as to LTP and STP of candidate 1 if elected.

To establish equilibrium, we consider four possible deviations from the equilibrium described in proposition 3.3.

First, suppose that candidate 2 deviates and offers $C_2(\beta_2)$ with $\beta_2 > \overline{\beta}$. The deviation is not profitable if candidate 2 is not elected; this, in turn, is only a best response for voters if candidate 1 chooses LTP when elected and reelected. This requires that the following inequality holds:

$$U_1^L(\overline{\beta}, RE) \geq U_1^S(NRE) \tag{3.30}$$

By construction $U_1^L(\overline{\beta}, RE) = U_1^S(NRE)$. Thus politician 2 will not be elected although he chooses LTP because candidate 1 demands less transfer and chooses LTP in accordance with our tie-breaking rule.

Second, suppose candidate 1 deviates to $C_1(\beta_1)$ with $\beta_1 < \overline{\beta}$. Such a deviation is only profitable if the public finds it in its best interests to elect and reelect him. Voters want to elect a candidate only if the candidate selects LTP once in office. Candidate 1 would choose LTP if the following inequalities hold:

$$U_1^L(\beta_1, RE) \geq U_1^S(NRE) \tag{3.31}$$

But $\beta_1 < \overline{\beta}$ implies directly $U_1^L(\beta_1, RE) < U_1^S(NRE)$; thus the public will elect candidate 2 because he undertakes LTP.

Third, suppose candidate 1 deviates to $C_1(\beta_1 V^2)$ with $\beta_1 > \overline{\beta}$. Then the public will not elect politician 1, even if he were to undertake LTP, because for voters the payments to the politician are lower when the second candidate is elected. Therefore the deviation is not profitable.

Finally, it is obvious that the second candidate has no incentive to offer a contract $C_2(\beta_2 V^2)$ with $\beta_2 < \overline{\beta}$, because he would receive lower transfers in the second period and in equilibrium can be sure of being elected anyhow.

Uniqueness follows in a similar way. For any offer constellation $C_1(\beta_1 V^2), C_2(\beta_2 V^2)$ with $\beta_i \neq \overline{\beta}$ for at least one candidate, one of the politicians has an incentive to deviate by offering $C_i(\overline{\beta}V^2)$or by offering an incentive contract that requires slightly fewer transfers from the public. [11]

□

[11] We omit the tedious but easy description of all possible cases.

4. Reelection Thresholds

4.1 Introduction

In this chapter we focus on a second potential shortcoming in democracies. We consider policies that have only short-term consequences. However, the randomness of future reelections may not provide politicians with sufficient motivation to devote a socially desirable amount of effort to certain policies. For example when the valuation of the effort allocation changes through shifting voter preferences, neither sanctions for deviations from the socially desirable amount of effort nor rewards for exerting the socially desirable amount of effort will be sufficiently high. The politician has then an incentive to choose the effort allocation according to his own preferences.

In this chapter we suggest that adding a threshold incentive contract to the election mechanism can increase social welfare of policies with short-term consequences without impairing the liberal principles of free and anonymous voting in democracies. A threshold incentive contract stipulates the minimum benefit or performance level a politician has to achieve in order to have the right to stand for reelection. Such threshold contracts may appear to reenforce the problem that the politician is not rewarded for his efforts in the future, since the probability of remaining in office decreases. However, when reelection chances are uncertain, social welfare can be increased through the incentive contract as deviations to lower efforts are punished more heavily.

The threshold incentive contract is equivalent to a conditional term limit imposed by the candidate on himself. Thus, it does not diminish the scope of the fundamental liberal principles of democracies of free and anonymous elections.

We consider a model in which an elected politician can exert effort on a public issue, one example could be institutional reforms. The effort creates benefits for the public. The politician's reelection chances increase with the created benefits. Since the politician is assumed to be motivated by holding the office, the uncertainty of the reelection chances does not provide the politician with sufficient motivation to exert socially optimal effort levels. In this chapter we consider a threshold incentive contract which the politician must accept upon election. We show that the dual mechanism - threshold incentive contracts and elections - can increase social welfare.

In this chapter, we assume that the voters use only partially retrospective criteria. They are also forward-looking. For instance, the competence and personal qualities of a competitor or communication skills and newly emerging issues in campaigns can influence the voting and elections (see e.g. Lupia and McCubbins (1998)). When voters are both backward- and forward-looking, we show that reelection thresholds can provide appropriate incentives.

It does not appear very difficult to introduce reelection thresholds in democracies. Threshold contracts would allow politicians to offer voters clear choices. Either a politician sticks to his campaign promise and can stand for reelection or he breaks his promise and that was his last term. In the famous example of when President George Bush announced "read my lips: no new taxes" threshold contracts would have not allowed him to abandon his campaign promise and then stand for reelection. Threshold contracts would have increased the commitment power of the promise if George Bush had wanted to commit himself to no increase of taxes. Another recent example where threshold contracts could have made a difference was the campaign promise of Chancellor Schröder to bring unemployment down to 3.5 million by 2002. With the opportunity of threshold contracts and competition between Schröder and the incumbent Kohl, either Schröder would have stopped short of making such promises or German voters could have been more confident that unemployment will actually decline in 2002. In short, adding reelection threshold contracts would turn cheap talk during campaigns into credible communication.

The chapter is organized as follows: In section 4.2 we outline the model. Section 4.3 presents the first-best solution. In section 4.4 we show how the reelection mechanism works. In section 4.5 we add the threshold incentive contract to the reelection mechanism and indicate the welfare implications. Section 4.6 concludes.

4.2 The Model

We consider the voters' problem of trying to motivate an elected politician. The voters and the politician are assumed to be risk-neutral. There are two periods. In the first period, the incumbent has to exert effort e on a task T, which for example could be the reform of the judiciary system. The effort e on task T creates benefits b for the public in the first period.[1] For simplicity, we assume

$$b = e. \tag{4.1}$$

The voters make their reelection decision dependent on their utility. From the perspective of the first period, however, the election at the beginning of the second period can be affected by many other factors than the realized benefit. Therefore, reelection is uncertain for the politician when he decides on his engagement. We assume that reelection chances can be summarized by a continuous probability function $p(b)$ that is known to the politician at the beginning of the first period. $p(b)$ is the probability that the politician will be reelected if the benefit b is realized and is given as

$$p(b) = \begin{cases} 0 & \text{for } b \le \underline{b}, \\ \gamma + \phi b & \text{for } \underline{b} \le b \le \bar{b}, \\ 1 & \text{for } b \ge \bar{b}, \end{cases}$$

with $-1 \le \gamma \le 0$, $\phi > 0$ and $\underline{b} \ge 0$. Furthermore, we assume in this example $\bar{b} \le e^{FB}$, where e^{FB} is the socially optimal effort. Note that in order to obtain $p(\bar{b}) = 1$ it is necessary that $\bar{b} = (1 - \gamma)/\phi$.

The fact that the reelection scheme is stochastic can be interpreted in several ways. For instance, while some voters may base their decision exclusively on the past performance of the politician, others may make their reelection decision dependent on other factors, such as leadership and communication skills of the

[1] Additional benefits may also materialize in the second period, but this has no bearing on our main results.

incumbent, or the perceived competence of a competitor emerging at the reelection stage, or on economic circumstances independent of current policies. Voter preferences may also shift, which induces noise at the reelection stage.

The utility of the politician, who acts as an agent for the voters is given by

$$U^A(b, e) = W_1 + p(b)W_2 - C(e). \tag{4.2}$$

W_1 denotes the utility of the office in period 1, W_2 the discounted utility of the office in period 2 and $C(e)$ the cost of exerting the effort in period 1. As the utility W_1 from office in the first period is sunk after the politician has been elected, it will be neglected in the subsequent analysis. The remaining utility takes the form

$$U^A(b, e) = p(b)W_2 - C(e). \tag{4.3}$$

Given the politician's utility, the participation constraint (PC) that the politician wants to stand for reelection amounts to

$$p(b)W_2 - C(e) \geq 0. \tag{4.4}$$

The politician chooses an effort level that maximizes his utility. Thus, the incentive constraint (IC) is given as:

$$e = \arg\max_e \{p(b)W_2 - C(e)\}. \tag{4.5}$$

For tractability, the cost $C(e)$ of the agent is assumed to be given as follows:

$$C(e) = ce^2. \tag{4.6}$$

The factor c can be interpreted in two ways. Either it measures the agent's disinclination to provide the effort e, or it could be interpreted as the competence of the politician, with small c meaning high competence, i.e., achieving a certain benefit level does not require much effort cost from the politician.

At the end of the first period, the benefits for the public are realized and the reelection decision takes place.

The overall game is summarized as follows:

Stage 1: Based on his reelection chances $p(b)$, the politician exerts his effort on task T.

Stage 2: The benefit from the politician's activity is realized. The public observes the benefit b and takes its reelection decision.

4.3 First-Best Solution

We first characterize the first-best solution, assuming that the public could commit itself to a reelection scheme, i.e. the electorate does not depend on $p(b)$ in designing contracts. We assume that the public enforces the socially optimal effort level directly by a contract heavily penalizing any deviation from the effort level prescribed in the contract. Hence the public's problem is to maximize its utility subject to the politician's participation constraint. The participation constraint must be honored by the public, because otherwise the politician would not seek reelection and would not enter into the contract. Since the PC must be taken into account, the reelection probability under a first-best solution must be equal to one. Otherwise, the public could demand a higher effort level, thereby still fulfilling the PC by increasing the reelection probability.

Hence, the voters' problem is given by

$$\max\{U^P = e\}, \tag{4.7}$$

$$s.t. \quad W_2 - C(e) \geq 0,$$
$$e \geq 0.$$

A simple Lagrange calculation leads to

Proposition 4.1
The first-best effort level is given by

$$e^* = \sqrt{\frac{W_2}{c}} \tag{4.8}$$

This is the maximum effort level the public can ask the politician to implement; higher effort levels would not satisfy the participation constraint and the politician would not seek reelection and forgo the contract.

4.4 The Reelection Mechanism

In this section we explore the sub-game perfect equilibria of the game if only the reelection mechanism is at work. The politician chooses his effort according to the incentive constraint (IC) as:

$$e = \arg\max_e \{p(b)W^2 - ce^2\}.$$

We obtain:

Proposition 4.2
Under the reelection scheme $p(b)$ the politician chooses his effort as

$$\begin{array}{llcll} (i) & e & = & 0 & \text{for } \frac{W_2}{c} < \frac{-4\gamma}{\phi^2} \\ (ii) & e^{int} & = & \phi\frac{W_2}{2c} & \text{for } \frac{-4\gamma}{\phi^2} \leq \frac{W_2}{c} \leq \frac{2(1-\gamma)}{\phi^2} \\ (iii) & e & = & \bar{b} & \text{for } \frac{W_2}{c} > \frac{2(1-\gamma)}{\phi^2} \end{array}$$

Proof of proposition 4.2

According to the IC, the politician chooses the effort level which maximizes his utility under the reelection scheme $p(b)$.

First, we observe $U^A(e) < U^A(\bar{b})$ for all $e > \bar{b}$. An effort level $e = \bar{b}$ guarantees reelection. It is obvious that the politician would never choose an effort level greater than the one required for sure reelection: effort levels greater than the one required would imply higher costs without additional benefits. Therefore, we can restrict the problem to

$$\max_e\{U^A(e)\}; \quad e \in [0; \bar{b}].$$

Either there is a corner solution, i.e., $e = 0$ or $e = \bar{b}$, or an interior solution.

In the interior solutions, the politician chooses his effort level according to the IC. The first-order condition implies

$$e^{int} = \phi\frac{W_2}{2c}$$

As

$$\frac{\partial^2 U^A}{\partial e^2} = \frac{\partial^2((\gamma + \phi b)W_2 - ce^2)}{\partial e^2} = -2c < 0,$$

only one utility maximum exists; it is given through the interior solution.

We now check in which cases the politician chooses the interior solution and in which cases he chooses one of the corner solutions.

The politician chooses $e = 0$ if $U^A(e^{int}) < U^A(0)$. This is given if

$$p(e^{int})W_2 - c(e^{int})^2 < 0$$

which can be written as

$$(\gamma + \phi\frac{\phi W_2}{2c})W_2 - c(\frac{\phi W_2}{2c})^2 < 0$$

which can be transformed into the condition

$$\frac{W_2}{c} < \frac{-4\gamma}{\phi^2}.$$

The politician chooses the upper corner solution when $e^{int} > \bar{b}$, because in this case the upper corner solution guarantees a higher utility. With $\bar{b} = (1-\gamma)/\phi$ we obtain the condition

$$\frac{W_2}{c} > \frac{2(1-\gamma)}{\phi^2}.$$

Thus, for

$$\frac{2(1-\gamma)}{\phi^2} \geq \frac{W_2}{c} \geq \frac{-4\gamma}{\phi^2}$$

the politician chooses the interior solution.

The interval is not empty if

$$\frac{2(1-\gamma)}{\phi^2} \geq \frac{-4\gamma}{\phi^2}$$

and thus if

$$-1 \leq \gamma$$

which is satisfied because of our assumption $-1 \leq \gamma \leq 0$.

The politician chooses $e = 0$ for $-4\gamma/\phi^2 > W_2/c$ and $e = \bar{b}$ for $2(1-\gamma)/\phi^2 < W_2/c$.

□

In most cases, the reelection mechanism creates inefficiencies compared to the first-best solution. The first-best solution would be implemented if $\bar{b} = e^*$ and $2(1-\gamma)/\phi^2 < W_2/c$. If $\bar{b} < e^*$ then first-best cannot be reached either because the politician can secure his reelection with an effort smaller than e^* or he may choose $e = 0$.

Proposition 4.2 allows for intuitive comparative statics. Suppose, e.g. we increase ϕ, the gradient of the reelection scheme, while we leave $\bar{b}$ constant through corresponding changes of γ. If the politician before had chosen the interior solution, the chosen effort increases as ϕ increases. Either, the interior solution increases or $e^{int} > \bar{b}$ and the politician switches to the upper corner solution.

The effort of the politician could be improved by committing to an adequate reelection mechanism. However, one of the fundamental principles of modern liberal democracy is free, anonymous and unconstrained voting at every election. Therefore, the stochastic element in $p(b)$ is a precondition for our analysis.

4.5 Threshold Incentive Contracts

In this section, we explore whether the introduction of a threshold incentive contract leads to a superior solution without impairing the liberal democracy principle of free and anonymous voting. We assume that there is an independent institution, for example a court, which has the same utility function as the voters and which has the right to decide whether or not the politician is allowed to stand for reelection. The reelection decision is given as follows: The court announces a threshold level $\hat{b}$ at the beginning of the first period. If the benefit realized at the end of the first period is smaller than $\hat{b}$, the politician cannot stand for reelection. If the benefit is equal to or higher than $\hat{b}$, the politician can stand for reelection. Then, the usual democratic election process with free and anonymous voting takes place. Thus, a hierarchy of incentive contracts and elections is formed. First, the decision is taken whether the politician has the right to stand for reelection, then the usual reelection mechanism takes place.

The overall game is summarized as follows:

Stage 0: A court prescribes a threshold level $\hat{b}$ that the politician has to reach if he wants to stand for reelection. The required level is known to the politician. Voters have a stochastic reelection scheme $p(b)$.

Stage 1: The politician exerts his effort on task T.

Stage 2: The benefit from the politician's activity is realized. If $b < \hat{b}$, the politician leaves office and does not stand for reelection. If $b \geq \hat{b}$ the politician stands for reelection and the reelection procedure takes place.

The politician's reelection probability changes to

$$p(e, \hat{b}) = \begin{cases} 0 & \text{for } b \leq \max[\underline{b}, \hat{b}], \\ \gamma + \phi b & \text{for } \max[\underline{b}, \hat{b}] \leq b \leq \bar{b}, \\ 1 & \text{for } b \geq \max[\bar{b}, \hat{b}]. \end{cases}$$

The politician chooses his efforts according to the modified incentive constraint, which now amounts to

$$e = \arg\max\{p(e, \hat{b})W_2 - ce^2\}.$$

Proposition 4.3

Again three types of solutions can occur in principle:

(i) $e = 0$ *(lower corner solution),*

(ii) $e = \max\{\bar{b}, \hat{b}\}$ *(upper corner solution),*

(iii) $e^{int}(\hat{b}) = \max\{\phi \frac{W_2}{2c}, \hat{b}\}$ *(interior solution).*

Proof of proposition 4.3

First, we rewrite the maximization problem of the politician under the hierarchy of incentive contracts and elections as

$$\max_e \{U^A(e, \hat{b})\}; \quad e \in [0; \max\{\bar{b}, \hat{b}\}]$$

As we know, three cases can occur. The lower corner solution remains the same with $e = 0$, but the upper corner solution changes into

$$e = \hat{b}$$

for $\hat{b} > \bar{b}$. Hence, the effort level in the upper solution is higher with a threshold incentive contract, or remains the same for $\hat{b} \leq \bar{b}$.

If $e^{int} \geq \hat{b}$, the politician exerts the effort e^{int}, because this is his utility maximizer. If $\hat{b} > e^{int}$ the politician will choose $e = \hat{b}$, because otherwise he is not reelected. He will not exert an effort $e > \hat{b}$ because $\partial U^A / \partial e > 0$ and $\partial^2 U^A / \partial e^2 < 0$ and e^{int} was the utility maximum.

□

The proposition indicates that the threshold incentive contract increases the upper corner solution and the interior solutions if an adequate threshold signal is stipulated. In the upper corner solution, the effort level can be raised by choosing a threshold signal $\hat{b} > \bar{b}$. In this case the effort level yielding sure reelection is $e = \hat{b}$. For the interior solutions, the effort level can be increased by choosing a threshold signal $\hat{b}$ with $\hat{b} > \phi W_2/2c$.

To derive the optimal threshold signal $\hat{b}^*$ we must ensure that $\hat{b}^*$ maximizes the chosen effort under the IC and that the PC is satisfied. We obtain

Proposition 4.4

The court chooses the threshold signal $\hat{b}^* = e^*$.

Proof of proposition 4.4

Obviously, $\hat{b}^* = e^*$ is the solution. The politician will not choose an effort level smaller than e^*, because then he would not be reelected. The participation constraint is satisfied because $U^A(e^*, e^*) = 0$. According to our tie-breaking rule, the politician chooses e^* and not $e = 0$.

□

In this model, the threshold incentive contract always leads to the first-best solution. It is thus welfare-improving if the politician chooses the interior solution under the reelection mechanism alone, or if $\bar{b} < e^*$ and the politician chooses the upper corner solution. Note that the assumption $\bar{b} \leq e^*$ is necessary because otherwise the reelection probability under the first-best effort level is smaller than one and the PC would not be satisfied. In this case, the optimal threshold signal would be the signal which fulfills $U^A(e(\hat{b}^*), \hat{b}^*) = 0$.

The threshold incentive contract works as follows: By giving the politician a threshold that he has to reach if he wants to stand for reelection, the court can force the politician to exert a higher effort than he would exert without the threshold.

One can extend the analysis by allowing politicians to offer threshold contracts during campaigns themselves. As shown in Gersbach and Liessem (2001) optimal contracts are offered if the politicians have the same competence, measured by their marginal costs of exerting effort. If the politicians differ in competence, then the politician with the higher competence will be elected.

4.6 Conclusion

Our analysis suggests that thresholds to reelection could be a viable supplementary mechanism to improve democratic procedures. Of course, there are a variety of practical issues involved in using incentive contracts in politics, as discussed in previous chapters for contracts stipulating money or utility transfers. Moreover, one might wonder whether a threshold contract as proposed in this chapter may lead to an underinvestment of effort on newly emerging issues, because they are not relevant for the right to stand for reelection. However, voters can still punish such behavior by not reelecting the politician. Moreover, one could introduce a clause that the contract is cancelled or renegotiated in the case of extraordinary events such as a war. Overall, however, the threshold contracts suggested in this chapter promise efficiency gains and might be the ones most easily introduced into politics.

5. Effort Incentives and Monetary Rewards

5.1 Introduction

In this chapter we examine the correlate to the problem dealt with in the last chapter. Instead of the randomness of future election outcomes, we consider measurability problems of policy outcomes that may lead to insufficient efforts of politicians to develop such policies. Instead of reelection thresholds, we focus in this chapter on how monetary rewards can alleviate incentive problems.

Democratic societies use elections and reelections to motivate politicians to choose efforts in accordance with the desire of voters. If the outcomes of tasks are difficult to measure and observe, this can make for a difficult motivation problem. Whereas the consequences of fighting unemployment or the consequences of fighting crime can be derived from the time series of a single number,[1] the outcomes from a reform of the health-care system or even of a redesign of the constitution are not measurable in simple figures or with any high degree of precision.

In this chapter, we first examine how the democratic election mechanism works for problems faced by politicians when outcomes are not precisely measurable. Second, we combine incentive

[1] Even in the case of unemployment there are considerable definitional problems, and real changes in unemployment can be obscured by changing definitions.

contracts for the politician and elections to improve the functioning of democracies. We show that it is beneficial to add an incentive contract which the politician must agree to in order to stand for reelection, even if all possible information about the performance of the politician is available to voters at election date.

We develop our argument by considering the model of an elected politician who exerts effort on a task creating benefits for the public. Voters observe a noisy signal of their benefits. At the end of the first period, the office holder stands for reelection. The voters decide on reelection by implementing a reelection scheme that depends on the observed signal or effort. The politician's effort incurs costs for him and he receives a fixed wage for each period he stays in office. We first investigate whether reelections alone are able to implement the social optimum. Later we supplement the reelection mechanism by an incentive contract in which the second-period wage is made flexible subject to a budget constraint.

Our main results are as follows: First, elections cannot provide sufficient incentives to implement the socially optimal solution when the benefit signal from a politician's effort is sufficiently noisy. The politician exerts less effort on the task than socially optimal. Even if the public can commit itself to a reelection scheme, the incumbent has an incentive to lower effort, since a higher level of effort has comparatively little impact on his reelection chances, while the costs accrue fully to the politician.

Second, we show that the combination of elections and incentive contracts for the politician leads to the socially optimal effort. An incentive contract stipulates wages in the first and second period subject to a budget constraint. The optimal incentive contract involves zero first-period wages and high second-period wages.[2] Together with a scheme that makes the reelection of the politician uncertain and thus may lower expected wage payments, the budget constraint can be fulfilled.

The combination (or hierarchy) of incentive contracts and reelection schemes eliminates the under-investment problem because the marginal benefit from exerting a unit of effort can be increased by paying a higher second-period wage. The associated reelection probability and the wage scheme satisfy the budget constraint but do not lower marginal benefits from making efforts. The incentive contract is self-financing and helps to solve the inefficiencies of the election mechanism, although the public does not have any more information about the politician's performance than it has under the scenario with elections alone.

Subsequently, we extend our analysis to wage caps on the remunerations of politicians and the inability of voters to commit themselves to a particular reelection scheme. We explore how the hierarchy of incentive contracts and elections can be used under such circumstances.

The chapter is organized as follows: In the next section we outline the model and our assumptions. In section 5.3, we identify the first-best solution. In section 5.4, we consider the potential and the limitations of the reelection mechanism in achieving the optimal solution. In section 5.5, we show that the combination of incentive contracts and reelection mechanism yields the social optimum. In

---

[2] Political science and the existing political economy models as a rule make the implicit assumption that being a politician is an attractive job because of perks associated with political office. In all of these models, however, exerting effort for a particular task is not the issue. We show how wages need to be determined in the first and second term in order to give the politician the best incentives to do a good job.

section 5.6, we explore the robustness of our results with respect to wage caps and the inability of voters to commit to a reelection scheme. Section 5.7 presents our conclusions.

5.2 The Model

We consider the voters' problem of trying to motivate an elected politician. The voters and the politician are assumed to be risk-neutral. There are two periods involved. In the first period, the incumbent has to exert effort e ($e \geq 0$) on a task denoted by T. This effort creates benefits B for the public. The benefits from the effort manifest themselves in the first period.[3] We assume

$$B = ke. \tag{5.1}$$

Factor k is the marginal benefit of a unit of effort exerted on task T.

The voters cannot observe B directly; instead, they receive the signal b about the benefits. In practice, the noise distorting the signal can be low or high. For example, if the politician invests his effort in the reduction of unemployment, the results at a particular time can be observed precisely by looking at the unemployment figures. Suppose, however, that the government reforms an inefficient judiciary system. This may provide utility gains over the next periods, but is very difficult to measure because benefits may be widespread and not identifiable in simple quantitative terms. In such cases, the benefit signal can be very noisy.

We assume that the benefit signal is given as:

[3] Additional benefits may also materialize in the second period, but this has no bearing on the functioning of our model.

$$b = ke + \epsilon. \tag{5.2}$$

The factor ϵ is a random variable assumed to be equally distributed on $[-a, a]$ with density function

$$f(\epsilon) = \frac{1}{2a}.$$

and distribution function

$$F(\epsilon) = \frac{\epsilon + a}{2a}.$$

Factor a represents the noise of the benefit signal. The parameter a is common knowledge. The expected utility for the public is denoted by U^P and given as:

$$U^P = E(B \mid b). \tag{5.3}$$

E is the expectation about the benefits, evaluated after the benefit signal b has been perceived. Given our assumption that the benefit signal b is determined by $b = B + \epsilon$, and thus $E(B \mid b) = b$, we can simply write

$$U^P = b. \tag{5.4}$$

An alternative interpretation would be that the public does not perceive a signal about its benefits, but that the benefits themselves are affected by shocks. This would model the situation of a politician who, say, exerts effort on a labor market reform, but the benefits of the effort are affected by macroeconomic shocks. In this case, the utility function is also given by $U^P = b$ but b now stands for the benefits for the public. Our results are valid for both perspectives on how noise makes it impossible for voters to precisely infer the effort of the politician. We will work with the first interpretation.

The voters make their reelection decision dependent on their expected utility and therefore on the observed signal. In order to give the reelection mechanism the best chance to motivate the politician, we assume that the voters offer a reelection scheme $p(b)$ to the politician at the beginning of the first period and that they are able to commit themselves to it.[4] $p(b)$ is the probability that the politician will be reelected if the benefit signal b was realized.

The expected utility of the politician is given by

$$\tilde{U}^A(b, e) = W_1 + q\{e \mid p(b)\}\delta W_2 - C(e). \tag{5.5}$$

W_1 denotes the utility of the office in period 1, W_2 the utility of the office in period 2 and $C(e)$ the cost of exerting the effort in period 1. $0 \leq \delta \leq 1$ is the discount factor of the politician. $q\{e \mid p(b)\}$ denotes the politician's expected reelection probability if he exerts the effort level e and the reelection scheme $p(b)$ is applied. To keep the following simple, we denote the expected reelection probability by $q(e)$ since $p(b)$ is given for every step of the analysis. Note that $q(e)$ is given by

$$q(e) = \int_{ke-a}^{ke+a} p(b)\frac{1}{2a}db. \tag{5.6}$$

The overall expected utility of office in period 2 is given by $q(e)\delta W_2$.

Note that the utility from holding office may include monetary benefits, such as a fixed wage, and non-monetary benefits, such as prestige or the desire to be in power.

The utility component W_1 from holding office in the first period is already fixed and therefore sunk with respect to the decision

[4] This assumption may be appropriate when all politicians are equal in terms of their cost and utility functions. Then the commitment of the voters to their reelection probability scheme may be credible. However, the commitment assumption mainly serves as a benchmark for our investigation.

regarding the effort. Thus, it will bc neglected in the subsequent analysis. Then, the utility function takes the form:

$$U^A(b, e) = q(e)\delta W_2 - C(e). \tag{5.7}$$

Given the utility function of the politician, the participation constraint (PC) amounts to

$$q(e)\delta W_2 - C(e) \geq 0. \tag{5.8}$$

The PC requires that the politician is better off by standing for reelection than by simply finishing his term and renouncing efforts on the task. The value of the outside option has been normalized to zero. Therefore the PC is always fulfilled by choosing $e = 0$. The politician chooses effort levels to maximize his utility, which is the incentive constraint (IC) voters face. Thus, the IC is given as:

$$e = \arg\max_e \{q(e)\delta W_2 - C(e)\}. \tag{5.9}$$

In order to break ties, we assume that a politician who is indifferent with respect to several actions will choose those which yield the highest utility for the voters.[5]

The costs $C(e)$ of the agent are assumed to be convex and given as follows:

$$C(e) = (ce)^2. \tag{5.10}$$

Recall that factor c can be interpreted in two ways. Either it is a parameter, that indicates the agent's cost of exerting effort, or it could be interpreted as the competency of the politician. Throughout this chapter we assume that the cost function is the same for all politicians.

[5] This assumption is made solely for simplicity of exposition.

At the end of the first period, the benefits for the public and the politician are realized. The public observes the benefit signal b and the reelection decision takes place.

The overall game is summarized as follows:

Stage 0: The voters commit themselves to a reelection scheme based on the observed benefit signal at the end of period 1.

Stage 1: The politician exerts his effort on the task T.

Stage 2: The benefits from all activities by the politician are realized. The public observes the benefit signal b and executes its reelection scheme.

5.3 First-Best Solution

We first characterize the first-best solution assuming that the public has perfect information about the agent's effort and enforces the socially optimal effort levels directly by a contract heavily punishing any deviation. Hence the voters' problem is to maximize their utility subject to the participation constraint of the politician. The participation constraint must be honored by the voters, because otherwise the politician would renounce the contract and leave office. Since voters must take the politician's PC into account, the reelection probability under a first-best solution must be equal to one. Otherwise, the public could demand higher effort levels, thereby still fulfilling the PC by increasing the reelection probability.

The perfect information assumption gives us

$$U^P = B. \tag{5.11}$$

Hence, the maximization problem is given by

$$\max\{U^P = ke\}, \tag{5.12}$$

$$\text{s.t.} \quad \delta W_2 - C(e) \geq 0,$$
$$e \geq 0.$$

Proposition 5.1

The first-best effort level is given by

$$e^* = \frac{\sqrt{\delta W_2}}{c} \tag{5.13}$$

Proof of proposition 5.1

As the politician's costs increase strictly in e, the problem of the voters is given by

$$\max\{U^P = ke\}$$
$$\text{s.t.} \quad \delta W_2 - (ce)^2 = 0$$
$$e \geq 0$$

which yields the solution of the problem as:

$$e^* = \frac{\sqrt{\delta W_2}}{c}$$

□

The first-best effort level depends on the politician's costs of undertaking the effort level e. The more costly an effort is, the less amount of effort the politician exerts.

5.4 The Reelection Mechanism

In this section we explore whether and under what conditions the reelection mechanism without incentive contracts is able to implement the first-best solution. We will show that even if the reelection scheme is designed optimally, first-best cannot be achieved if the noise of the benefit signal is sufficiently high. We use subgame perfect implementation, i.e. we look at reelection schemes and subgame perfect equilibria of the overall game that yield the first-best solution.

We investigate this topic using a threshold reelection scheme defined as

$$p(b) = \begin{cases} 1 & \text{if } b \geq \hat{b}, \\ 0 & \text{otherwise.} \end{cases} \tag{5.14}$$

The politician is reelected with certainty if his benefit signal is above a certain threshold level, denoted by $\hat{b}$ where $\hat{b}$ is assumed to be greater than zero. If he fails to achieve the required benefit signal, he will not be reelected. We denote by $U^A(\hat{b}, e)$ the expected utility of the politician if the public uses the threshold $\hat{b}$ and the agent exerts effort e.

This reelection scheme has the best chance of motivating the politician, because the marginal benefits of an additional unit of effort are higher than under any other reelection scheme.[6] Accordingly, once the first-best solution is reached, the politician has the lowest incentives to deviate to smaller effort levels. Thus, there is

[6] This follows from the observation that for all expected reelection probabilities $\tilde{q}(b)$, the marginal increase in the reelection chance cannot exceed the density of the noise and thus: $\frac{\partial \tilde{q}}{\partial e} |_e \leq \frac{k}{2a}$.

no other reelection scheme that yields a better solution. Therefore our results are valid for all other classes of reelection schemes. To simplify notation, whenever we use the expression $q(e)$ in the following analysis, we will be referring to a threshold reelection scheme.

The expected reelection probability denoted by $q(e)$, can be written as:

$$q(e) = \begin{cases} 0 & \text{if } \hat{b} - ke \geq a, \\ 1 - F(\hat{b} - ke) = 1 - \dfrac{\hat{b} - ke + a}{2a} & \text{if } -a < \hat{b} - ke < a, \\ 1 & \text{if } \hat{b} - ke \leq -a. \end{cases}$$

The expected reelection probability is zero if the politician exerts an effort level e that is too low, meaning that the threshold signal can never be reached. The expected reelection probability is $1 - F(\hat{b} - ke)$ if the politician exerts an effort level e for which the threshold signal can be achieved with a certain degree of probability. Finally, reelection is certain if the politician chooses an effort level e generating a signal that is definitely above $\hat{b}$. We obtain:

Proposition 5.2
Under the threshold reelection scheme $p(b)$ only three choices for effort levels are possible:

(i) $e^{l-cor} = 0$, *(lower corner solution)*

(ii) $e^{u-cor} = \dfrac{\hat{b} + a}{k}$ *(upper corner solution)*

(iii) $e^{int} = \dfrac{1}{4ac^2} k\delta W_2$ *(interior solution)*

Proof: see appendix.

Note that the interior solution is only defined if the associated solution e^{int} fulfills $-a < \hat{b} - ke^{int} < a$. In the following, we show that the reelection mechanism is able to implement the first-best solution for small values of the noise parameter a, but generates inefficiencies for larger values of a.

Proposition 5.3

If $a \leq \bar{a}$, the threshold scheme

$$p^*(b) = \begin{cases} 1 \text{ if } b \geq b^* := ke^* - a \\ 0 \text{ otherwise} \end{cases}$$

implements the first-best solution. The critical value $\bar{a}$ is given by

$$\bar{a} = \frac{k\sqrt{\delta W_2}}{4c}$$

Proof: see appendix.

The reasoning of the proposition is simple: if the politician chooses the first-best effort level e^*, his participation constraint is only satisfied by a reelection probability of one. According to proposition 5.2, the required benefit signal is chosen such that the politician will choose e^* under the upper corner solution. This benefit signal is denoted by b^*. Since the first-best effort level can only be implemented if the politician chooses the upper corner solution, we have to check whether he has an incentive to deviate to the interior solution and to the lower corner solution $e = 0$. This is not the case for $a \leq \bar{a}$, because for $a \leq \bar{a}$ the interior solution does not exist and the politician has also no incentives to choose $e = 0$ since reelection chances would be zero.

In the next stage, we determine the threshold reelection scheme which is second-best if $a > \bar{a}$. Second-best choices are denoted by $p^o(b)$, b^o and e^o.

Proposition 5.4
For $a > \bar{a}$, a second-best reelection scheme is given by

$$p^o(b) = \begin{cases} 1 & \text{if } b \geq b^o \text{ and } a + \frac{k^2 \delta W_2}{8ac^2} \geq b^o > \max\{\frac{k^2 \delta W_2}{4ac^2} - a; a\} \\ 0 & \text{otherwise} \end{cases}$$

with the effort level

$$e^o = e^{int} = \frac{1}{4ac^2} k \delta W_2.$$

Proof: see appendix.

In the proof we show that there is no threshold reelection scheme implementing for $a > \bar{a}$ an effort level e that is higher than the effort level chosen under the interior solution, because the politician would always deviate either to the interior solution or to $e = 0$. Thus, any reelection scheme that implements e^{int} is second-best. Note that we have indeterminacy with respect to the second-best reelection scheme in the sense that b^o is not unique. Note that b^o must be chosen such that the PC is fulfilled.

The reelection scheme in proposition 5.4 is still of the threshold type but a first-best effort level cannot be achieved anymore since $e^{int} = 1/(4ac^2) k \delta W_2 < e^* = \sqrt{\delta W_2}/c$ for $a > \bar{a} = (k\sqrt{\delta W_2})/4c$.

The comparative statics of the effort level chosen under the second best reelection scheme are given as follows

Corollary 5.1

$$(i)\ \frac{\partial e^o}{\partial a} < 0 \qquad (ii)\ \lim_{a \to \infty} e^o = 0$$

The reasons are as follows: as the noise of the effort increases, the marginal benefit of exerting a unit of effort diminishes, since a higher level of effort has only little effect on the politicians reelection chances, while the costs accrue fully to the politician.

5.5 Self-Financing Incentive Contracts

In this section, we assume that voters can supplement their reelection scheme by an incentive contract. If he wants to stand for reelection, a politician must accept an incentive contract in the first period stipulating a certain wage level in periods 1 and 2. The incentive contract allows the public to base the politician's utility in the second period on variables observed in the first period. Throughout this section, this is assumed to occur via monetary transfers dependent on the benefit signal achieved. To focus exclusively on the differential impact of monetary transfers, we normalize all other components of the utility to zero, such as the desire to appear competent or statesman-like. Thus, in this section, W_1 and W_2 stand for the additional utility a politician derives from monetary transfers in periods 1 and 2, respectively. The governmental actions are constrained by a fixed budget which can be used over two periods for wage payments to politicians in office. Therefore, an incentive contract must be self-financing in the sense that the associated expected wage payments cannot be larger than a fixed amount. We will show that the combination of incentive contracts and elections can implement the first-best solution.

The modified structure of the game is as follows:

Stage 0: The voters commit themselves to a reelection scheme based on the signal observed at the end of period 1.

Stage 0': The politician signs the incentive contract if he wants to stand for reelection.

Stage 1: The politician exerts his effort on task T.

Stage 2: The benefits from all the activities of the politician are realized. The public observes the benefit signal b and executes its reelection scheme.

The introduction of incentive elements implies that the fixed wages assumed in the previous sections here become variable. Therefore, we relax the assumption of fixed and equal wages in each period and instead assume that an overall budget constraint must be fulfilled for the expected wage expenditures and thus for the incentive contracts.

We use $\overline{W}$ to denote the expected amount paid to the politicians in both periods.[7] The public's budget constraint is:

$$W_1{}^{inc} + \frac{q(e)}{1+r} W_2{}^{inc} + \frac{(1-q(e))}{1+r} W_1{}^{inc} = \overline{W}. \tag{5.15}$$

$W_1{}^{inc}$ and $W_2{}^{inc}$ are the wages paid in the first and second periods under the "incentive contract scenario"[8] and r denotes the interest rate. Note that if the incumbent is not reelected, a new politician is paid according to $W_1{}^{inc}$. The fact that the budget constraint can be formulated in expected terms rests on the risk neutrality of the government and the public, respectively.

We first examine the optimal wage allocation over both periods in the first-best solution. The first-best effort level was obtained

[7] Note that $\overline{W}$ could be determined endogenously as well by stipulating an overall objective function, since our results are valid for arbitrary values of $\overline{W}$.

[8] The superscript "inc" is used throughout the section as indicator for the variables under the "incentive contract scenario".

under the assumption that the public could enforce the desired effort level under the restriction of the participation constraint.

From proposition 5.1, it immediately follows that an increase of the wage in period 2, W_2, leads to a higher first-best effort level e^*. Accordingly, it is optimal to set ${W_2}^{inc}$ as follows:

$$ {W_1}^{inc} = 0, \quad {W_2}^{inc} = \frac{\overline{W}(1+r)}{q(e)}. \tag{5.16} $$

Equation (5.16) is an optimality condition.[9]

Under flexible wages, we therefore obtain the first-best solution

$$ e^{*inc} = \frac{\sqrt{\delta \overline{W}(1+r)}}{c}. \tag{5.17} $$

As $q(e)W_2^{inc} = \overline{W}(1+r)$, the first-best solution can be achieved by any positive reelection probability if W_2^{inc} is adjusted accordingly.

Now we examine whether the combination of a threshold reelection scheme $p(b)$ and a variable second-period wage ${W_2}^{inc}$ can implement the first-best solution. We first obtain:

Proposition 5.5

For $a \leq \bar{a}^{inc}$, the threshold reelection scheme

$$ p^{*inc}(b) = \begin{cases} 1 \text{ if } b \geq b^{*inc} := ke^{*inc} - a \\ 0 \text{ otherwise} \end{cases} $$

and the wage announcement ${W_2}^{inc} = \overline{W}(1+r)$ lead to the first-best solution. The critical value $\bar{a}^{inc}$ is given by

$$ \bar{a}^{inc} = \frac{k\sqrt{\delta \overline{W}(1+r)}}{4c} $$

[9] If there is a fixed minimum wage ${W_1}^{inc}$ payable to the politician in the first period, or if a new politician can not be paid according to ${W_1}^{inc}$, the incentive contract must be adjusted accordingly.

Proposition 5.5 replicates the result in proposition 5.3. If the measurement error, captured by the value a, is sufficiently small, the first-best solution can be implemented. The proof follows the same logic as the proof of proposition 5.3 and is therefore omitted here.

Now we investigate whether the combination of threshold schemes and flexible wages can implement the first-best solution for $a > \bar{a}^{inc}$. In contrast to the fixed wage scenario, we obtain:

Proposition 5.6
For $a > \bar{a}^{inc}$, the combination of the wage

$$W_2{}^{inc} = \frac{4ac\sqrt{\overline{W}(1+r)}}{\sqrt{\delta k}}$$

and the threshold reelection scheme

$$p^{o,inc}(b) = \begin{cases} 1 & \text{if } b \geq b^{o,inc} := a + \dfrac{k}{2c}\sqrt{\delta \overline{W}(1+r)} \\ 0 & \text{otherwise} \end{cases}$$

implements the first-best solution.

Proof: see appendix.

Proposition 5.6 is the major result of this chapter. The reasoning for the result is as follows: To achieve the first-best solution for $a > \bar{a}^{inc}$, the effort level under the reelection scheme $p^{o,inc}(b)$, denoted by $e^{o,inc}$, must be the first-best effort level e^*. This yields a condition on $W_2{}^{inc}$. The budget constraint of the public and the participation constraint of the politician are satisfied if the expected wage payment in period 2 is equal to $\overline{W}$. This is the case if $q(e)W_2{}^{inc} = \overline{W}(1+r)$. The threshold scheme $p^{o,inc}(b)$ satisfies this condition. The incentive contract works because we can enlarge the marginal benefit of a unit of effort by increasing the wage in the second period. The optimal reelection probability is smaller than one, because the budget constraint of the public must be fulfilled. Nevertheless, the uncertain reelection does not destroy the possibility of creating first-best incentives because the marginal return on efforts depends on the level of second-period wages. Clearly, to motivate the politician second-period wages need to be increased. The subtle question is: Can effort be increased such that no costs in expected terms arise for the public. For wages to increase, the reelection probability must decline necessarily. The whole point of this chapter is that this decline of reelection chances can be engineered in a way that first-best solutions can be achieved.

A more general alternative to model the budget constraint would be to introduce welfare costs $\lambda(W)W$ of the wages. $\lambda(W)$ could, for example, measure the tax distortion. Since all decisions take place in the first period, expected welfare costs matter. Thus, for $\lambda(W) = \lambda = const$ minimizing expected welfare costs yields the same result as in this chapter. If $\lambda(W)$ is increasing in W because tax rates increase, the high second-period wages may not be optimal and the first-best solution may not be feasible. There are alternative means of how politicians can get high benefits if they are reelected, for example pay-backs and other private perks associated with continued incumbency in office which also enter the government budget constraint. In this respect this chapter provides an argument that private benefits granted after a politician has been reelected have a positive incentive component. However, since the reelection probability must decline to achieve a first-best outcome this argument is a subtle and important twist on this general point.

5.6 Robustness and Non-commitment

In this section we explore the robustness of our results with respect to the key assumptions of our model. First, we discuss what happens if the budget of the government is limited within a period, and second we relax the assumption that the voters can commit themselves to a reelection scheme.

Suppose that the government is restricted in its wage payment for the second period. The limitation of wages could arise because of increasing tax distortions when very high wages are paid to a politician or due to popular concerns about "excessive" compensation of politicians. As a consequence, the government may not be able to pay ${W_2}^{inc}(a)$ for large values of the noise a and the first-best solution cannot be reached. Nevertheless, as e^{int} is given as

$$e^{int} = \frac{1}{4ac^2} k\delta W_2,$$

even a small increase of W_2 raises the effort and thus a better solution can be achieved than under the reelection mechanism alone. A shifting of wage payments from the first to the second period and thus a higher second period wage always has positive effects on effort and welfare. Thus, even if the budget of the government is limited, social welfare can be increased by adding incentive contracts to elections.

The assumption that voters can commit to a reelection scheme has been made in order to give the reelection mechanism the best chance to motivate politicians. However, in liberal democracies voters cannot commit themselves or future citizens to adhere to a particular voting behavior. The commitment problem is rooted in the uncertainty about interests of future voters and in the liberal principle of democracies to allow for free and anonymous voting behavior in every election.

We can integrate the inability of commitment in a simple way into our model.

Suppose for instance the reelection mechanism is given by

$$p(b) = \begin{cases} 1 & \text{if } b \geq \hat{b} + \eta, \\ 0 & \text{otherwise.} \end{cases} \tag{5.18}$$

The factor η is a random variable with density function $f(\eta)$ and mean $E(\eta) = 0$. η can be interpreted as an exogenous shock on the reelection chances of the politician representing future shifts of electoral preferences or the emergence of attractive competitors. Thus, the benefit signal that the politician has to reach in order to be reelected itself becomes noisy.

The shock on the reelection chances can be interpreted as additional noise to the benefit signal. Therefore, the analysis of this non-commitment problem follows the analysis in the sections before. However, the probability distributions are more general because the noise of the benefit signal is given by $\epsilon - \eta$ instead of ϵ in the previous sections and $\epsilon - \eta$ will not be uniformly distributed.[10] A second period wage $W_2{}^{inc}(a)$ can be found under which the politician exerts the first-best effort levels. While this incentive contract is still self-financing in most cases, there are some special cases in which additional payments have to be made.[11]

---

[10] Even if η is also uniformly distributed, we obtain a triangular distribution.

[11] While first-best can always be achieved, it is an open issue for which classes of probability distributions self-financing contracts exist. Examples are available upon request.

There might be a second and more extreme case of non-commitment when voters reject the incumbent at the reelection date with certainty in order to save future remunerations for the politician. In this case, the nature of incentive contracts can be amended in the following way. The incentive contract, i.e. the wage payment ${W_2}^{inc}(a)$ becomes effective if the politician reaches the optimal required benefit signal $\hat{b}$, regardless of whether he is reelected or not. Thus, he can receive the wage payments even if he is not in office anymore. Such contracts therefore need a golden parachute clause.

5.7 Conclusion

The major result of this chapter suggests that when politicians face tasks of which the outcomes are not measurable with precision, democratic societies might do better to add an incentive contract to the reelection mechanism. It is clear that the present model is only the first step in integrating effort problems into the hierarchy of incentive contracts and elections. Most importantly, since politicians face many tasks simultaneously how can the hierarchy of incentive contracts and elections be extended to complex multi-task settings? In Gersbach and Liessem (2003) it is indicated that the hierarchy can still work in multi-task environments by using incentive contracts on particular tasks, while the performance across all tasks is assessed in the election.

5.8 Appendix

Proof of proposition 5.2

The solution $e = 0$ occurs when reelection probability $q(0)$ provides the highest utility for the politician. In this case, the politician does not exert any effort at all, because the benefits of exerting any amount of effort are always lower than the costs involved.

The solution

$$e = \frac{\hat{b} + a}{k}$$

occurs if the politician maximizes his utility by certain reelection. A reelection probability of one requires effort levels $e \geq (\hat{b}+a)/k$. We call this solution the "upper corner solution". It is obvious that the politician would never choose effort levels greater than the ones required for certain reelection: effort levels greater than the one needed for sure reelection would imply higher costs and no additional benefits.

The third solution

$$e = \frac{1}{4ac^2} k\delta W_2$$

occurs if the politician maximizes his utility by choosing his effort level e from the range $-a < \hat{b} - ke < a$. His reelection probability in this case is $1 - F(\hat{b} - ke)$. The incentive constraint amounts to:

$$e = \arg\max_{e} \{(1 - F(\hat{b} - ke))\delta W_2 - (ce)^2\}.$$

The first-order condition implies

$$kf(\hat{b} - ke)\delta W_2 - 2c^2 e = 0,$$

and the politician exerts the effort

$$e = \frac{1}{4ac^2} k\delta W_2$$

This completes the proof.

□

Proof of proposition 5.3

If the politician chooses the first-best effort level e^* his participation constraint is only satisfied with a reelection probability of one. Hence, if the politician chooses the upper corner solution, the optimal threshold reelection scheme must implement the first-best effort level e^*. According to proposition 5.2 it is sufficient to choose the required threshold signal $\hat{b}$ such that

$$e^* = \frac{\hat{b} + a}{k},$$

which requires that

$$\hat{b} = b^* = ke^* - a.$$

The utility of the politician is zero.

First-best can be implemented if IC and PC are satisfied under the reelection scheme $p^*(b)$ and the effort level e^*. Since the PC is fulfilled by construction, the IC remains to be checked. The politician should have no incentive to deviate to the interior solution or to the solution $e = 0$ under the threshold scheme $p^*(b)$.

We first show that for $a \leq \bar{a}$ the interior solution does not exist. The critical condition $-a < b^* - ke^{int}$ amounts to:

$$-a < k\frac{\sqrt{\delta W_2}}{c} - a - k\frac{k\delta W_2}{4ac^2}$$

Solving for a yields

$$a > \bar{a} = \frac{k\sqrt{\delta W_2}}{4c}$$

Hence, for $a \leq \bar{a}$, the interior solution does not exist.

In the second step we show that the politician will never choose the solution $e = 0$. Choosing $e = 0$ implies that the signal b lies in $[-a, a]$. We observe that $q(0) > 0$ requires $p^*(a) = 1$ which holds if and only if $a > ke^* - a$ or $2a > ke^*$. This is equivalent to

$$a > \frac{k\sqrt{\delta W_2}}{2c},$$

which contradicts our assumption

$$a \leq \frac{k\sqrt{\delta W_2}}{4c}.$$

Note that the politician has zero utility from choosing $e = 0$. Because of our tie-breaking rule the politician will choose e^*. Therefore, if $a \leq \bar{a}$, the first-best solution can be implemented.

□

Proof of proposition 5.4

The proof proceeds in two steps. First, we derive the optimal threshold reelection scheme within the class of schemes that lead to the interior solution. Second, we show that no other threshold reelection scheme yields higher utility for the public.

We claim that when the interior solution is the optimal choice of the politician, the optimal threshold reelection scheme must belong to the class

$$p^o(b) = \begin{cases} 1 & \text{if } b \geq b^o \text{ and } a + \dfrac{k^2\delta W_2}{8ac^2} \geq b^o > \max\{\dfrac{k^2\delta W_2}{4ac^2} - a; a\} \\ 0 & \text{otherwise} \end{cases}$$

The optimal threshold reelection scheme has to satisfy $U^A(e^{int}) \geq 0$ and thus

$$\left(1 - F(b^o - ke^{int})\right)\delta W_2 - (ce^{int})^2 \geq 0$$

which is satisfied if

$$\left(1 - \frac{b^o - \frac{1}{4ac^2}k^2\delta W_2 + a}{2a}\right)\delta W_2 - \left(\frac{1}{4ac}k\delta W_2\right)^2 \geq 0$$

which can be transformed to

$$\frac{\delta W_2}{2} - \frac{b^o \delta W_2}{2a} + \frac{k^2\delta^2 W_2^2}{16a^2c^2} \geq 0$$

which is equivalent to

$$b^o \leq a + \frac{k^2\delta W_2}{8ac^2}.$$

On the other hand it must hold

$$1 - F(b^o - ke^{int}) < 1$$

which holds if and only if

$$ke^{int} - a < b^o$$

which is equivalent to

$$b^o > k^2\frac{1}{4ac^2}\delta W_2 - a.$$

Furthermore it must be $q(0) = 0$ and thus $b^o > a$.

Thus, within the range $a + \frac{k^2\delta W_2}{8ac^2} \geq b^o > \max\{\frac{k^2\delta W_2}{4ac^2} - a; a\}$, the threshold b^o can be freely chosen without inducing the politician to leave the interior solution as long as the reelection scheme is of the threshold type.

For $a = \bar{a}$ the upper and lower boarder for b^o coincide in the value $\frac{3k}{4c}\sqrt{\delta W_2}$. This is of course, the same value as the threshold b^* reaches in proposition 5.3, when $a = \bar{a}$ is inserted. For $a > \bar{a}$ the upper boarder is strictly above the lower boarder and as we have the assumption $a > \bar{a}$ in proposition 5.4, there is always a positive difference between the upper and the lower boarder for b^o in this case.

In the second step, we show that no other threshold scheme can yield a higher utility for voters. The only alternative is a threshold scheme which leads to a corner solution. Suppose a threshold scheme can implement an effort level $e^{u-cor} = \frac{(\hat{b}+a)}{k} = e^o + \zeta$ for some $\zeta > 0$ under the corner solution. This would require a minimum benefit signal $b = k(e^o + \zeta) - a$.

The participation constraint would be satisfied because the politician is reelected with certainty and $e^{int} + \zeta \leq e^*$.

A necessary condition to satisfy the IC for the upper corner solution under consideration is

$$U^A\left(k(e^o + \zeta) - a, e^o + \zeta\right) \geq U^A\left(k(e^o + \zeta) - a, e^o\right).$$

This is satisfied if

$$\delta W_2 - (c(e^o + \zeta))^2 \geq \left(1 - \frac{ke^o + k\zeta - a - ke^o + a}{2a}\right)\delta W_2 - (ce^o)^2$$

and thus if

$$\frac{k\zeta}{2a}\delta W_2 \geq c^2(2e^o\zeta + \zeta^2)$$

which yields

$$\zeta^2 + 2e^o\zeta - \frac{k\zeta}{2ac^2}\delta W_2 \leq 0.$$

Using the equilibrium value

$$e^o = \frac{1}{4ac^2} k \delta W_2$$

we obtain the condition:

$$\zeta^2 \leq 0.$$

Therefore, the IC is not fulfilled and the politician will always deviate, which completes the proof.

□

Proof of proposition 5.6

To achieve the first-best solution under $a > \bar{a}^{inc}$, the effort level must coincide with e^{*inc}. This is equal to the condition:

$$\frac{1}{4ac^2} k \delta {W_2}^{inc} = \frac{\sqrt{\delta \overline{W}(1+r)}}{c}$$

and therefore the second-period wage must fulfill:

$${W_2}^{inc} = \frac{4ac}{\delta k} \sqrt{\delta \overline{W}(1+r)} = \frac{4ac}{\sqrt{\delta k}} \sqrt{\overline{W}(1+r)}$$

To satisfy the budget constraint, ${W_2}^{inc}$ must fulfill:

$$q(e) {W_2}^{inc} = \overline{W}(1+r),$$

which imposes a condition on the required benefit signal $b^{o,inc}$. This condition amounts to:

$$\left(1 - F(b^{o,inc} - ke^{*inc})\right) {W_2}^{inc} = \overline{W}(1+r),$$

which implies

$$\left(1 - \frac{b^{o,inc} - ke^{*inc} + a}{2a}\right) {W_2}^{inc} = \overline{W}(1+r).$$

Therefore, the benefit signal is given by:

$$b^{o,inc} = ke^{*inc} - \frac{2a\overline{W}(1+r)}{W_2{}^{inc}} + a.$$

Inserting $W_2{}^{inc} = \frac{4ac}{\sqrt{\delta k}}\sqrt{\overline{W}(1+r)}$ and $e^{*inc} = \frac{\sqrt{\delta\overline{W}(1+r)}}{c}$ yields:

$$b^{o,inc} = a + \frac{k}{2c}\sqrt{\delta\overline{W}(1+r)}.$$

The budget constraint of the public is satisfied for this signal by construction.

The participation constraint of the politician amounts to

$$\left(1 - F(b^{o,inc} - ke^{*inc})\right)\delta W_2{}^{inc} \geq (ce^{*inc})^2,$$

which can be rewritten as

$$\delta\overline{W}(1+r) \geq (ce^{*inc})^2 = \delta\overline{W}(1+r).$$

since $e^{*inc} = \frac{\sqrt{\delta\overline{W}(1+r)}}{c}$. Thus, the participation constraint is always satisfied.

Finally, the first-best solution can be implemented if there is a guarantee that the reelection probability under the effort level e^{*inc} for the given benefit signal $b^{o,inc}$ is smaller than one and greater than zero.

$q(e) > 0$ is equivalent to $b^{o,inc} - ke^{*inc} < a$ which yields

$$a - \frac{k}{2c}\sqrt{\delta\overline{W}(1+r)} < a.$$

This is always satisfied for $k > 0$ and $\delta\overline{W}(1+r) > 0$.

The reelection probability $q(e)$ is smaller than one if

$$b^{o,inc} - ke^{*inc} > -a.$$

Inserting $b^{o,inc}$ yields the condition

$$a - \frac{k}{2c}\sqrt{\delta\overline{W}(1+r)} > -a.$$

which can be transformed to $a > \frac{k}{4c}\sqrt{\delta\overline{W}(1+r)} = \overline{a}^{inc}$. This condition is fulfilled by assumption.

□

6. Limits to Incentive Contracts in Politics

6.1 Introduction

In this section we provide a simple example why the enthusiasm portrayed in this part for the hierarchy of incentive contracts and elections might not be without limits. In particular, when politicians can propose their own wage for each term they are in office, adverse consequences might occur.[1] There are two sorts of concerns.

First, wealthy candidates for office may be able to renounce compensation by the public completely and hence other, less wealthy candidates, may not be able to compete on equal terms in political campaigns. This may undermine the thrust in a democracy that the pool of candidates for political positions should not be *a priori* constrained.

Second, allowing politicians to compete on their compensation terms without any constraints might not lead to higher welfare than fixed and predetermined wages: either because wage costs for the public increase and/or somewhat less competent politicians will be elected. In the following we provide a simple example for this second issue.

[1] However, it is also premature to call for legal limits. In the opposite direction, Eichenberger (2001) e.g. argues for a wide ranging abolishment of regulations in politics.

Our example draws on two strands of literature. First, candidates will provide a public good if they hold office and thus we may face the standard free riding and underprovision problem when public goods are privately supplied, which is studied e.g. in Palfrey and Rosenthal (1984), Bergstrom, Blume, and Varian (1986), Mailath and Postlewaite (1990), Güth and Hellwig (1986) and recently Hellwig (2001). Through setting wages or by allowing politicians to offer compensation schemes, the public can overcome the underprovision problem in our model.

Second, we use a version of citizen-as-candidates models, developed by Osborne and Slivinski (1996) and Besley and Coate (1997). In such settings citizens who consider running for office must trade off their private costs and policies they would like to undertake with benefits from policies other potential candidates are likely to implement.

There is a recent literature on how paying politicians affects the set of citizens to run for office. Besley (2004) examines how paying politicians can solve agency problems of incumbents who are subject to a two-period term-limit. Caselli and Morelli (2004) examine how the quality of elected politicians is affected by the value of office when candidates know in advance whether they can convince the electorate of their abilities. Messner and Polborn (2003) develop a new type of citizen-candidate model by assuming that the abilities of candidates are observable by voters, but their opportunity costs are private information. Poutvaara and Takalo (2003) develop a tractable citizen-candidate model that allows for unobserved ability differences, informative campaigning and political parties. In particular the last three of these recent advances in modeling representative democracies illustrate that increasing the value of office does not necessarily increase the average qual ity of candidates. None of the preceding papers focus, however, on the comparison between remuneration set by the public and self-designed wages as we set out in this chapter.

This chapter is organized as follows. In the next section we introduce the model. Then we examine fixed wages set by the public. In section 6.4 we identify equilibria when politicians can propose their own remunerations. Section 6.5 contains the welfare comparisons and section 6.6 concludes.

6.2 The Model

We consider a society with N voters who have to elect a politician who undertakes policy projects for all members of the group. There are two potential candidates, $i = 1, 2$, for this job. The remaining $N - 2$ individuals cannot be candidates and only act as voters.[2] Candidates differ in their competence: Candidate i ($i = 1, 2$) can generate a net benefit b_i ($b_i > 0$) by his policies for every member of the society. We label candidates such that $b_1 \geq b_2$. We assume that the benefits candidates can generate for each member of the society are observable.

For each candidate i, there is an individual cost c_i of serving in office. This cost includes the opportunity cost and any non-monetary gains from being in office. If the latter source of utility is more important we have $c_i < 0$. c_i is assumed to be perfectly observable by the voters.[3]

[2] We assume that N is greater than 4 and thus there are more voters who do not seek office than candidates.

[3] A fruitful extension of the model is to assume positive costs of campaigning and standing for election.

The politician receives a compensation denoted by $W \geq 0$, which is financed by distortionary taxation levied on all other members of the society. Let $\lambda > 0$ denote the shadow cost of public funds. That is, taxation uses $(1 + \lambda)$ of tax payers' resources in order to levy 1 unit of resources for paying wages to candidates in office. The utility of candidate i if he is elected politician is

$$b_i + W - c_i, \tag{6.1}$$

and the utility of any other member of the society is

$$b_i - \frac{W(1 + \lambda)}{N - 1}. \tag{6.2}$$

If no potential candidate is willing to run, then a default policy will be implemented that yields a benefit of $b_0 = 0$ for every voter. If only one candidate runs for office, then he automatically assumes power. We examine two scenarios. In the first scenario, we examine how voters would determine the wages for politicians.

The timing in the first scenario is as follows:

Stage 1: The voters decide about the height of the compensation W of the politician.

Stage 2: The candidates decide simultaneously whether to run for office or not.

Stage 3: The voters elect one of the two candidates.

It is obvious in this first scenario that, if both candidates run for office, it is always optimal for the voters to elect candidate 1, because $b_1 \geq b_2$ and wages for both candidates are identical.

In the second scenario candidates themselves can offer wages, denoted by W_1 and W_2, which become effective if a candidate runs and will be elected. Therefore, in the second scenario the first two stages are replaced by:

Stage 1′: Candidates offer W_1 and W_2.

Note that it is always possible for a candidate to propose a compensation so large that he will never get elected. Therefore we do not explicitly model a stage where candidates decide whether to run or not.

6.3 Fixed Wages

We look at the first scenario. We will neglect equilibria in weakly dominated strategies. Then we obtain our first result.

Proposition 6.1
There exists an equilibrium for stages 2 and 3 that depends on the level of compensation in the following way:

- *If* $W \geq c_2 - b_2$ *and*
$$W \geq \frac{N-1}{N+\lambda}(c_1 - (b_1 - b_2))$$
then candidate 1 runs for office and is elected.
- *If* $W \geq c_2 - b_2$ *and*
$$W < \frac{N-1}{N+\lambda}(c_1 - (b_1 - b_2))$$
then candidate 2 runs for office and is elected.
- *If* $W < c_2 - b_2$ *and* $W \geq c_1 - b_1$*, then candidate 2 does not run for office. Candidate 1 runs for office and is elected.*
- *If* $W < c_2 - b_2$ *and* $W < c_1 - b_1$ *no candidate runs for office.*

Proof

Note that if candidate 1 decides to run for office, he will be elected, independently of whether candidate 2 decides to run for office or not. Therefore, candidate 2 should run for office if and only if his utility from serving as a politician is greater than zero, which is his utility from the default outcome. Thus, the strategies "run for office if $b_2 + W - c_2 \geq 0$" and "do not run otherwise" are (weakly) dominant for candidate 2. Hence, if $W \geq c_2 - b_2$, candidate 2 runs for office. If $W \geq c_2 - b_2$, then candidate 1 runs for office if

$$b_1 + W - c_1 \geq b_2 - \frac{W}{N-1}(1+\lambda)$$

and thus if his utility from holding office is higher than the utility when candidate 2 governs. The condition can be transformed into

$$W \geq \frac{N-1}{N+\lambda}(c_1 - (b_1 - b_2))$$

If $W < c_2 - b_2$, candidate 1 runs for office if $b_1 + W - c_1 \geq 0$ and thus if $W \geq c_1 - b_1$. □

Proposition 6.1 indicates that high wages can attract the more competent politician to run for office.[4] We will later determine optimal wage levels the public should set for the political race.

6.4 Competition for Wage Contracts

In this section we explore what happens if candidates can offer to perform political duties for a certain wage. After the candidates have proposed their remuneration scheme, the voters elect the

[4] The equilibrium is unique if we eliminate weakly dominated strategies.

candidate which creates the highest utility for them. Thus, the timing is as follows:

Stage 1′: Each candidate proposes a remuneration scheme W_i.

Stage 2: The voters elect one of the two candidates

The wage offers W_1 and W_2 are common knowledge of candidates and voters. Note that we can neglect the decision of candidates to run for office since they can propose arbitrarily high wages. We first observe that candidate 1 is elected if [5]

$$b_1 - \frac{W_1}{N-1}(1+\lambda) \geq b_2 - \frac{W_2}{N-1}(1+\lambda) \tag{6.3}$$

We first look at the equilibrium in which candidate 1 is elected.

Proposition 6.2

If $(1+\lambda)(c_1 - c_2) \leq (N+\lambda)(b_1 - b_2)$ *there exists an equilibrium in which candidate* 1 *is elected with wage offers that satisfy:*

$$W_1 = (b_1 - b_2)\frac{N-1}{1+\lambda} + W_2$$

Proof

First note that in order for candidate 1 to be elected, W_1 must satisfy

$$W_1 \leq (b_1 - b_2)\frac{N-1}{1+\lambda} + W_2$$

because otherwise the public is better off by electing candidate 2. This follows from equation (6.3). Therefore, when candidate 1 wants to be elected he offers the wage

$$W_1 = (b_1 - b_2)\frac{N-1}{1+\lambda} + W_2. \tag{6.4}$$

5 For convenience, we will use a tie-breaking rule in all propositions in favor of the elected candidate in equilibrium.

A downwards deviation can be excluded, because then candidate 1 could rise his utility by offering a higher wage and would still be elected. A deviation to a higher wage leads to the election of candidate 2.

Candidate 1 will not deviate to a higher wage than in 6.4 and will not leave the office to candidate 2 if

$$b_1 + W_1 - c_1 \geq b_2 - \frac{W_2}{N-1}(1+\lambda).$$

Inserting the equilibrium value of W_1 as a function of W_2 from equation (6.4) this condition becomes

$$b_1 + (b_1 - b_2)\frac{N-1}{1+\lambda} + W_2 - c_1 \geq b_2 - \frac{W_2}{N-1}(1+\lambda)$$

which can be transformed into

$$(b_1 - b_2)\left(1 + \frac{N-1}{1+\lambda}\right) + W_2\left(1 + \frac{1+\lambda}{N-1}\right) \geq c_1$$

which yields

$$W_2 \geq \frac{N-1}{N+\lambda}c_1 - (b_1 - b_2)\frac{N-1}{1+\lambda} \tag{6.5}$$

Thus, candidate 1 wants to run for office if condition (6.5) is fulfilled and hence the proposed remuneration W_2 passes a certain threshold.

We next examine the optimal choice of W_2 by candidate 2. A possible deviation from the proposed equilibrium in the proposition for candidate 2 would be to offer a wage $W_2' = W_2 - \epsilon$ which would lead to his election. Candidate 2 will not choose this option if

$$b_1 - \frac{W_1}{N-1}(1+\lambda) \geq b_2 + W_2' - c_2$$

and thus if his utility from being citizen under candidate 1 is higher than his utility from holding office himself. By inserting the equilibrium value of W_1 which is given by (6.4) we obtain the condition

$$b_1 - \frac{W_2}{N-1}(1+\lambda) - (b_1 - b_2) \geq b_2 + W_2 - \epsilon - c_2$$

which can be transformed into

$$W_2 \leq \frac{N-1}{N+\lambda}(c_2 + \epsilon). \tag{6.6}$$

Therefore, if the wage W_2 is small enough, candidate 2 wants rather to be a citizen under candidate 1 than standing for office with a lower wage.

Therefore, there exist values for wage offers W_2 which satisfy both conditions (6.5) and (6.6) only if

$$\frac{N-1}{N+\lambda} c_2 \geq \frac{N-1}{N+\lambda} c_1 - (b_1 - b_2)\frac{N-1}{1+\lambda}$$

and hence we obtain the assumption of the proposition given by:

$$(1+\lambda)(c_1 - c_2) \leq (N+\lambda)(b_1 - b_2)$$

□

An important feature of proposition 6.2 is that wages are indeterminate, i.e. there are infinitely many combinations of pairs (W_1, W_2) that can constitute an equilibrium. As a corollary we obtain by using conditions (6.4), (6.5) and (6.6):

Corollary 6.1
Suppose $(1+\lambda)(c_1 - c_2) < (N+\lambda)(b_1 - b_2)$.

Then there exists an equilibrium in which candidate 1 is elected with minimal wages W_1^{min} and W_2^{min} given by:

$$W_2^{min} = \frac{N-1}{N+\lambda} c_1 - (b_1 - b_2)\frac{N-1}{1+\lambda}$$
$$W_1^{min} = \frac{N-1}{N+\lambda} c_1$$

There also exists an equilibrium in which candidate 1 is elected with maximal wages W_1^{max} and W_2^{max} given by

$$W_2^{max} = \frac{N-1}{N+\lambda} c_2$$
$$W_1^{max} = (b_1 - b_2)\frac{N-1}{1+\lambda} + \frac{N-1}{N+\lambda} c_2$$

In the next step we look at equilibria in which candidate 2 wins. Proposition 6.2 and corollary 6.1 indicate that candidate 1 can ask for higher wages than candidate 2. The wage difference is of course closely related to the additional benefits $b_1 - b_2$ candidate 1 will generate for voters.

Proposition 6.3
For $(1+\lambda)(c_1 - c_2) > (N+\lambda)(b_1 - b_2)$ there exists an equilibrium in which the candidate 2 is elected with wage offers W_1 and W_2 that satisfy:

$$W_1 = (b_1 - b_2)\frac{N-1}{1+\lambda} + W_2$$

The proof of proposition 6.3 follows the lines of the proof of proposition 6.2 and is therefore omitted.

6.5 Welfare Comparisons

In this section, we establish welfare comparisons for the case $c_2 = 0$ and $b_2 \geq 0$ to illustrate potential drawbacks of competitively offered wage schemes by politicians. Following the logic of chapter 6.3, in the case of a fixed wage candidate 2 will run for office for any wage $W \geq 0$ because $b_2 + W \geq 0$. Candidate 1 will enter the political competition if

$$W \geq \tilde{W} := \frac{N-1}{N+\lambda}\left(c_1 - (b_1 - b_2)\right)$$

where we have denoted the critical wage level by $\tilde{W}$.

If $\tilde{W} < 0$, then the welfare maximizing wage under a fixed remuneration scheme, which is denoted by W^{opt}, is zero. Candidate 1 runs for office for any non-negative wage W and is elected with certainty. Therefore the public sets $W^{opt} = 0$, because otherwise they had to incur the wage costs.

Overall welfare, denoted by U^{fix}, is given by

$$U^{fix} = Nb_1 - c_1 - \lambda W^{opt} = Nb_1 - c_1.$$

If $\tilde{W} > 0$, there exist two potentially optimal wage offers. The first of these wage levels is $W^{opt} = 0$, in which case candidate 1 would not run for office and candidate 2 would be elected. In this case overall welfare would be given by $U^{fix} = Nb_2$.

The second potentially optimal wage level is $W^{opt} = \tilde{W}$. In this case, candidate 1 would run for office and would be elected with certainty. Overall welfare would be given as: $U^{fix} = Nb_1 - c_1 - \lambda\tilde{W}$. Therefore, for $\tilde{W} > 0$, $W^{opt} = \tilde{W}$ is the optimal remuneration for politicians, if $Nb_1 - c_1 - \lambda\tilde{W} \geq Nb_2$.

We next turn to compensation schemes competitively offered by the politicians. According to section 6.4, candidate 1 offers the wage

$$W_1 = (b_1 - b_2)\frac{N-1}{1+\lambda} + W_2$$

and is elected, if $(1+\lambda)\, c_1 < (N+\lambda)(b_1 - b_2)$.

Candidate 2 would not deviate in this case from a wage W_2 if $W_2 \leq c_2(N-1)/(N+\lambda)$. As $c_2 = 0$ this requires $W_2 = 0$. Thus $W_2 = 0$ is the equilibrium compensation scheme by candidate 2 and the equilibrium wage of candidate 1 is therefore given by:

$$W_1 = (b_1 - b_2)\frac{N-1}{1+\lambda}.$$

The overall welfare, denoted by U^{var}, is given in this case by:

$$U^{var} = Nb_1 - c_1 - \lambda\frac{N-1}{1+\lambda}(b_1 - b_2).$$

For $(1+\lambda)\, c_1 > (N+\lambda)(b_1 - b_2)$ candidate 2 is elected with a wage W_2 which must satisfy the equilibrium boundaries. Overall welfare is simply:

$$U^{var} = Nb_2 - \lambda W_2.$$

We now examine different cases:

Case 1: Suppose $\tilde{W} < 0$. This implies $c_1 < b_1 - b_2$ which can be easily verified by checking the definition of $\tilde{W}$. Then $(1+\lambda)c_1 < (N+\lambda)(b_1 - b_2)$ holds. Therefore, candidate 1 is elected under competition for wages with $W_2 = 0$ since $W_2^{max} = 0$, and welfare is given by

$$U^{var} = Nb_1 - c_1 - \lambda\frac{N-1}{1+\lambda}(b_1 - b_2).$$

Under a fixed wage we have

$$U^{fix} = Nb_1 - c_1.$$

Thus, welfare is higher under the fixed wage scenario.

Case 2: Suppose $\tilde{W} > 0$ and $(1+\lambda)\,c_1 < (N+\lambda)(b_1 - b_2)$. Then candidate 1 is elected under competition for wages. Since $W_2^{max} = 0$, welfare in this case is given by:

$$U^{var} = Nb_1 - c_1 - \lambda \frac{N-1}{1+\lambda}(b_1 - b_2).$$

Under a fixed wage welfare depends on which candidate is elected and thus

$$U^{fix} = \max\left\{Nb_1 - c_1 - \lambda\tilde{W}, Nb_2\right\}.$$

Welfare is higher under a fixed wage scenario because

$$\tilde{W} < \frac{N-1}{1+\lambda}(b_1 - b_2)$$

Case 3: Suppose $\tilde{W} > 0$ and $(1+\lambda)\,c_1 > (N+\lambda)(b_1 - b_2)$. In this case candidate 2 is elected under competitive wages. The welfare under competition for wages is given by

$$U^{var} = Nb_2 - \lambda W_2.$$

Under the fixed wage framework welfare is

$$U^{fix} = \max\left\{Nb_1 - c_1 - \lambda\tilde{W}, Nb_2\right\}.$$

Hence, welfare is higher than under competitive wages.

We summarize the comparison between fixed and self-designed remunerations as follows:

Proposition 6.4

For $\lambda > 0$, welfare is always higher under fixed wages than under competitive wages, and monotonically decreasing in λ.

Proposition 6.4 is our main result and can be explained as follows. In principle, welfare can be lower because less competent candidates are elected or wage costs, and therefore tax distortions are higher. The comparisons in the cases illustrate that under competitive wage offers by candidates, realized wage costs become higher than under fixed and predetermined remunerations for politicians. The main reason is that wage competition by politicians bids up wages, because externalities for the other candidate and for all voters are not taken into account. One can also show that the competence of politicians tends to be higher when wages are set by the public (see Gersbach (2004b)).

6.6 Conclusion

In this chapter we have expressed some caution with respect to the dual mechanism if politicians can simply compete on compensation packages. In Gersbach (2004b), a more elaborate analysis of the model in this chapter broadly supports this conclusion. Nevertheless, the caution might not be as serious as it appears to be from looking straight at the model.

First, wages set by the public must be tailored such that the welfare-maximizing candidate runs and will be elected. Second, higher wage costs under competitively offered compensation schemes may be negligible in the government budget. Nevertheless, at this stage allowing for competitively offered wages in each term is not the most important priority in broadening the scope of democracies.

Epilogue to Part I

The first part of the book has advanced the both provocative and canonical idea that the dual mechanism of contracts and elections should be allowed to operate in liberal democracies. The dual mechanism can transform democracies in a fundamental way. Here we consider not only the efficiency gains identified so far and the new role of informational intermediaries in politics, but also the improved democratic procedures that are themselves welfare-improving. The transformation of democracies from a state where election campaigns are subject to a situation in which candidates are compelled to make many promises, most of which will remain unfulfilled, to a state where candidates are held accountable for these promises is a worthwhile goal in the attempt to improve liberal democracies.

References to Part I

ALESINA, A., and H. ROSENTHAL (1995): *Partisan Politics, Divided Government, and the Economy.* Cambridge University Press, Cambridge.

ALESINA, A., and G. TABELLINI (1990): "A Positive Theory of Fiscal Deficits and Government Debt," *Review of Economic Studies*, 57(3), 403–414.

ARROW, K. (1951): *Social Choice and Individual Values.* Yale University Press, New Haven.

BARON, D., and J. FEREJOHN (1989): "Bargaining in Legislatures," *American Political Science Review*, 83(4), 1181–1206.

BARRO, R. (1973): "The Control of Politicians: An Economic Model," *Public Choice*, 14, 19–42.

BEN-PORATH, Y. (1975): "The Years of Plenty and the Years of Famine – a Political Business Cycle?," *Kyklos*, 28(2), 400–403.

BERGSTROM, T., L. BLUME, and H. VARIAN (1986): "On the Private Provision of Public Goods," *Journal of Public Economics*, 29, 25–49.

BERNHOLZ, P. (1997): "Property rights, contracts, cyclical social preferences and the Coase theorem: A synthesis," *European Journal of Political Economy*, 13, 419–442.

——— (1999): "The generalized Coase Theorem and separable individual preferences: an extension," *European Journal of Political Economy*, 15, 331–335.

BERNHOLZ, P., and F. BREYER (1993): *Grundlagen der Politischen Ökonomie.* Mohr.

BESLEY, T. (2004): "Paying Politicians: Theory and Evidence," *Journal of the European Economic Association*, 2, 193–215.

BESLEY, T., and S. COATE (1997): "An Economic Model of Representative Democracy," *Quarterly Journal of Economics*, 112, 85–114.

——— (1998): "Sources of Inefficiency in a Representative Democracy: a Dynamic Analysis," *American Economic Review*, 88(1), 139–156.

BLACK, D. (1958): *The Theory of Committees and Elections.* Cambridge University Press, Cambridge, MA.

BLEICKEN, J. (1991): *Die athenische Demokratie.* UTB, Paderborn.

BUCHANAN, J., and G. TULLOCK (1965): *The Calculus of Consent: Logical Foundations of Constitutional Democracy.* University of Michigan Press.

BUCHANAN, J., and R. WAGNER (1977): *Democracy in Deficit.* Academic Press, New York.

CASELLI, F., and M. MORELLI (2004): "Bad Politicians," *Journal of Public Economics*, 88, 759–782.

COHEN, L., and R. NOLL (1990): "The Political Discount Rate," *Technical Paper No. 209, Stanford University, Center for Economic Policy Research.*

CUKIERMAN, A., and A. MELTZER (1986): "A Positive Theory of Discretionary Policy: The Cost of a Democratic Government and the Benefits of a Constitution," *Economic Inquiry*, 24, 367–388.

DIXIT, A. (1995): *The Making of Economic Policy: A Transaction Costs Politics Perspective.* MIT Press, Cambridge, MA.

DOWNS, A. (1957): *An Economic Theory of Democracy.* Harper and Row, New York.

DRAZEN, A. (2000): *Political Economy in Macroeconomics.* Princeton University Press, Princeton, New Jersey.

EICHENBERGER, R. (2001): "Economic Innovations Depend Upon Political Innovations: On Deregulating the Political Process," *Working Paper, University of Fribourg.*

ENELOW, J., and M. HINICH (1984): *The Spatial Theory of Voting: An Introduction.* Cambridge University Press, Cambridge.

FEREJOHN, J. (1986): "Incumbent Performance and Electoral Control," *Public Choice*, 50, 5–25.

FREY, B. (1983): *Democratic Economic Policy. A Theoretical Introduction.* Oxford University Press, New York.

GERSBACH, H. (1993): "Politics and the Choice of Durability: Comment," *American Economic Review*, 83(3), 670–673.

——— (2003): "Incentive Contracts and Elections for Politicians and the Down-Up Problem," in *Advances in Economic Design*, ed. by M. Sertel, and S. Koray. Springer-Verlag, Berlin.

——— (2004a): "Competition of Politicians for Incentive Contracts and Elections," *Public Choice.*

——— (2004b): "Competition of Politicians for Wages and Office," *CEPR Discussion Paper*, 4261.

GERSBACH, H., and T. KLEINSCHMIDT (2004): "Designing Democracies for Sustainability," University of Heidelberg, (mimeo).

GERSBACH, H., and V. LIESSEM (2001): "Reelection Threshold Contracts in Politics," *CESifo Working Paper*, 622.

——— (2003): "Incentive Contracts and Elections for Politicians with Multi-Task Problems," *CEPR Discussion Paper*, 4074.

GLAZER, A. (1989): "Politics and the Choice of Durability," *American Economic Review*, 79(5), 1207–1213.

GÜTH, W., and M. HELLWIG (1986): "The Private Supply of a Public Good," *Journal of Economics/Zeitschrift für Nationalökonomie*, 5, 121–159.

HART, O. (1995): *Firms, Contracts and Financial Structure*. Clarendon Press, Oxford.

HELLWIG, M. (2001): "The Impact of the Number of Participants on the Provision of a Public Good," *Working Paper, University of Mannheim*.

HIBBS, D. J. (1977): "Political Parties and Macroeconomic Policy," *American Political Science Review*, 71, 1467–1497.

——— (1992): "Partisan Theory after Fifteen Years," *European Journal of Political Economy*, 8, 361–373.

HOLMSTRÖM, B., and P. MILGROM (1991): "Multitask Principal-Agent Analyses: Incentive Contracts, Asset Ownership, and Job Design," *Journal of Law, Economics, and Organization*, 7, 24–52.

INMAN, R., and M. FITTS (1990): "Political Institutions and Fiscal Policy: Evidence from the US Historical Record," *Journal of Law, Economics and Organization*, 6, 79–132.

JENSEN, H. (1997): "Credibility of Optimal Monetary Delegation," *American Economic Review*, 87, 911–920.

KLEINHEYER, G. (1968): *Die kaiserlichen Wahlkapitulationen. Geschichte, Wesen und Funktion*. C.F. Müller, Karlsruhe.

LEBLANC, W., J. J. SNYDER, and M. TRIPATHI (2000): "Majority-Rule Bargaining and the Underprovision of Public Investment Goods," *Journal of Public Economics*, 75, 21–47.

LIESSEM, V. (2002): "Incentive Contracts for Politicians: A Viable Supplement to Democracies," *Working Paper, University of Heidelberg*.

LIPSET, S. M. (1995): *The Encyclopedia of Democracy*. Congressional Quarterly, Washington D.C.

LOCKWOOD, B. (1997): "State-Contingent Inflation Contracts and Unemployment Persistence," *Journal of Money, Credit, and Banking*, 29, 286–299.

LOHMANN, S. (2003): "Why Do Institutions Matter? An Audience Cost Theory of Institutional Commitment," *Governance*, 16(1), 95–110.

LOTTES, G. (2000): "Zwischen Herrschaftsvertrag und Verfassungsnotariat. Die Wahlkapitulationen der deutschen Kaiser und Könige.," in *Reich, Regionen und Europa in Mittelalter und Neuzeit. Festschrift für Peter Moraw.*, ed. by P. Heinig, S. Jahns, H. Schmidt, R. C. Schwinges, and S. Wefers, pp. 133–148. Historische Forschungen. 67, Berlin.

LUPIA, A., and D. MCCUBBINS (1998): *The Democratic Dilemma.* Cambridge University Press, Cambridge.

MAILATH, G., and A. POSTLEWAITE (1990): "Asymmetric Information Bargaining Procedures with Many Agents," *Review of Economic Studies*, 57, 351–367.

MERKEL, W., H. PUHLE, A. CROISSANT, C. EICHER, and P. THIERRY (2003): *Defekte Demokratien: Theorien und Probleme, Band 1.* Leske + Budrich, Opladen.

MESSNER, M., and M. POLBORN (2003): "Paying Politicians," *Journal of Public Economics, forthcoming.*

MUELLER, D. (1989): *Public Choice II.* Cambridge University Press, Cambridge.

NISKANEN, W. (1971): *Bureaucracy and Representative Government.* Chicago: Aldine-Atherton.

NORDHAUS, W. (1975): "The Political Business Cycle," *Review of Economic Studies*, 42, 169–190.

OLSON, M. (1965): *The Logic of Collective Action.* Harvard University Press, Cambridge, MA.

——— (1982): *The Rise and Decline of Nations.* Yale University Press, New Haven, CT.

OSBORNE, M., and A. SLIVINSKI (1996): "A Model of Political Competition with Citizen-Candidates," *Quarterly Journal of Economics*, 111, 65–96.

PALFREY, T., and H. ROSENTHAL (1984): "Participation and the Discrete Provision of Public Goods," *Journal of Public Economics*, 24, 171–193.

PERSSON, T., G. ROLAND, and G. TABELLINI (1997): "Separation of Powers and Political Accountability," *Quarterly Journal of Economics*, 112, 1136–1202.

PERSSON, T., and L. SVENSSON (1989): "Why a Stubborn Conservative Would Run a Deficit: Policy with Time-Inconsistent Preferences," *Quarterly Journal of Economics*, 104(2), 325–345.

PERSSON, T., and G. TABELLINI (1993): "Designing Institutions for Monetary Stability," *Carnegie-Rochester Conference Series on Public Policy*, 39, 53–84.

——— (2000): *Political Economics: Explaining Economic Policy.* MIT Press, Cambridge, MA.

POUTVAARA, P., and T. TAKALO (2003): "Candidate Quality," *CESifo Working Paper*, 1106.

POZZA, M. (1997): "Wahlkapitulationen," in *Lexikon des Mittelalters, Band 8*, ed. by N. Angermann, pp. 1914–1918. LexMA-Verlag, München.

ROGOFF, K. (1990): "Equilibrium Political Budget Cycle," *American Economic Review*, 80(1), 21–36.

SCHMIDT, M. (2000): *Demokratietheorien.* Leske + Budrich, Opladen.

SEN, A. (1970): *Collective Choice and Social Welfare.* Holden-Day, San Francisco.

STIGLITZ, J., and A. HEERTJE (1989): *The Economic Role of the State.* Blackwell, Oxford, UK.

SVENSSON, L. (1997): "Inflation Forecast Targeting: Implementing and Monitoring Inflation Targets," *European Economic Review*, 41, 1111–1146.

TABELLINI, G., and A. ALESINA (1990): "Voting on the Budget Deficit," *American Economic Review*, 80(1), 37–49.

TOLLISON, R. (1982): "Rent Seeking: A Survey," *Kyklos*, 4, 575–602.

VIERHAUS, R. (1977): *Herrschaftsverträge, Wahlkapitulationen, Fundamentalgesetze.* Max-Planck-Institut für Geschichte, Göttingen.

WALSH, C. (1995a): "Optimal Contracts for Central Bankers," *American Economic Review*, 81, 150–167.

——— (1995b): "Price Stability as the Objective of Monetary Policy and Recent Central Bank Reforms," in *NBER Macroeconomics Annual 1995*, ed. by B. Bernanke, and J. Rotemberg.

WEINGAST, B. (1981): "The Political Economy of Benefits and Costs: A Neoclassical Approach to Distributive Politics," *Journal of Political Economics*, 89(4), 642–664.

WITTMAN, D. (1995): *The Myth of Democratic Failure - Why Political Institutions Are Efficient.* University of Chicago Press, Chicago.

Part II

Rules for Decision-Making and Agenda Setting

7. Overview

7.1 The Ideas

In Part Two, we present a series of suggestions as to how a society can design decision rules, agenda rules, and agenda setter rules. The suggestions will be developed under the umbrella of constitutional economics and democratic mechanisms. As an illustration, consider a society which decides on either the allocation of a public project or the division of resources among its citizens. There are four types of inefficiencies:

- inefficient projects are proposed and adopted,
- efficient projects are proposed but rejected,
- efficient projects are not proposed,
- inefficient redistribution proposals are adopted.

Moreover, democratic processes may violate certain fairness criteria. We present a number of ideas for remedying these shortcomings.

Decision Rules

Decision rules prescribe how individual voting decisions are to be translated into outcomes for a society. We consider:

- Flexible Majority Rules
  Majority rules are flexible if the size of the majority depends on the proposal. For instance, the size of the majority may depend on the share of taxed individuals in a public project allocation problem, or the required majority may depend on the distribution of resources among individuals.
- Double Majority Rules
  The community is divided into two non-empty groups. Double majority rules require that a proposal be accepted in both groups by a prespecified share of supporting votes.

Agenda Rules

Agenda rules act as constraints. Violating the constraints makes an agenda unconstitutional, and the status quo prevails. Examples of agenda rules are:

- maximal taxation of the agenda setter: the agenda setter pays the maximal tax rate proposed in his agenda;
- no subsidies: the agenda setter is not allowed to propose any subsidies;
- taxation constrained to majority winners: only majority winners can be taxed;
- the financing package must satisfy the budget constraint;
- amendment rights for the opposition;

- exclusion of repeated agenda setting: the individual allowed to design the agenda in the first period is excluded from agenda setting in the second period.

Agenda Setter Rules

Agenda setter rules describe how the agenda setter will be treated after he has made proposals and voting has taken place. Examples of agenda setter rules are:

- Costs of Agenda Setting
  The agenda setter must pay a fixed amount if his agenda does not lead to the provision of a public project.
- Flexible Costs of Agenda Setting
  The agenda setter has to pay a fixed amount if his proposal does not lead to the provision of a public project. Additionally, he pays a variable amount if the share of supporting votes is less than a certain percentage.

In the next chapters we will illustrate that

the appropriate combination of decision rules, agenda rules, and agenda setter rules can yield first-best allocations of public projects in democracies;

the appropriate combination of decision rules, agenda rules, and agenda setter rules can help to achieve an efficient and fair division of resources.

7.2 The Theme

We develop our arguments and ideas within the framework of constructive constitutional economics, as outlined in the classical contribution by Buchanan and Tullock (1965), and surveyed by Mueller (1989) and Cooter (2000). In line with a long tradition dating back at least to Rousseau (1763), (see also Wicksell (1896), and Harsanyi (1955)), Buchanan and Tullock (1965) have examined the costs and benefits of majority rules that a society chooses behind a veil of ignorance. Aghion and Bolton (1998) have introduced contractual incompleteness for the design of optimal majority rules. We develop new democratic decision rules which, together with agenda rules and agenda setter rules, can transcend the limitations of democracies in achieving desired outcomes.

We develop our analysis within a democratic implementation framework into which we introduce the liberal democracy constraint in the following sense. The constitutional principles assumed must fulfill the fundamental democratic principles of equal voting and agenda rights. Moreover, constitutional principles cannot require more messages from citizens than proposals or voting. Thus, democratic constitutions are understood as the liberal democracy constraint on the set of all feasible mechanisms for collectively providing public projects, or distributing resources among individuals in a society.

When we allow for asymmetric information regarding the utilities individuals receive from public projects, our analysis is closely related to the fundamental issues in mechanism design. Two main results in the area of mechanism design represent polar cases for our analysis. First, d'Aspremont and Gérard-Veret (1979) and Arrow (1979) show that the expected externality mechanism as a direct revelation mechanism yields an *ex post* efficient social choice if agents must participate. Second, the Myerson-Satterthwaite theorem (Myerson and Satterthwaite (1983)) shows that there is no Bayesian incentive-compatible social-choice function that is efficient *ex post* if agents are free to opt out of the mechanism. We introduce democratic mechanisms where people are forced to participate, everyone has an opportunity to set the agenda, and only yes/no messages (voting) are allowed. Therefore, from a mechanism design viewpoint, it is not clear *a priori* whether democratic mechanisms are efficient.

Our work also draws upon collective choice theory, pioneered by Arrow (1951), and developed and summarized among others by Downs (1957), Black (1958), Riker (1962), Sen (1970), Schwartz (1986), Ordeshook (1986), Bernholz and Breyer (1993), and Saari (1995). In our models, the focus is restricted to two alternatives. This allows us to circumvent the difficulties presented by social choice theory. It remains to be seen how the concepts developed here can be embedded in more general approaches to social choice.

Part Two is organized as follows: In the next chapter, we introduce new agenda rules using simple examples. In chapter 9, we show how flexible majority rules in combination with agenda rules and agenda setter rules can help to achieve first-best allocations of public projects. In chapter 10, we extend our analysis to unobservable utilities that require a mechanism design framework; first-best mechanisms may then need double majority rules and flexible agenda costs. Finally, we show how flexible majority rules, supplemented by agenda rules, can guarantee an efficient and envy-free distribution of resources.

8. Examples for Agenda Rules[1]

8.1 Introduction

In this chapter we develop constitutional principles for democracies on how to treat individuals when a society decides on public project provision and financing. Such rules place constraints on the set of admissible agendas and are therefore called agenda rules. We introduce such agenda rules by simple examples.

At the constitutional stage, a society decides how public project provision and financing should be governed in the legislative periods under a veil of ignorance. We use the broad term public project that encompasses public goods. Individuals do not know at the constitutional stage whether they will benefit from the public project. Beneficiaries at the legislative stage are called project winners. Those individuals who suffer from the public project are called project losers. The set of project losers can be empty. In many cases, however, public projects can affect part of the society negatively. Examples of the latter category are the downsizing of the defense industry after the end of the cold war, labor market reforms that put pressure on wages for some workers or even the construction of roads, which may increase the noise for the resi-

[1] An extended version of this chapter has appeared in Gersbach (2004b).

dents living close to them. *A priori* there is no reason to assume that there are no project losers.

The constitutional principles in this chapter and in the whole part must obey liberal democracy's fundamental principles of equal voting and agenda rights. Moreover, constitutional principles cannot require more messages from citizens than proposals or voting including the possibility of non-participation.

Given these democratic constraints we consider a series of examples of constitutional principles that are at the disposition of the society. Decision rules are m–majority rules with $\frac{1}{2} \leq m \leq 1$. We assume open ballots, and hence individuals can be divided *ex post* into majority winners and minority losers.

Examples for agenda rules are: taxation or subsidization constrained to winners or losers of the majority voting process or equal treatment of majority winners or losers with respect to net transfers (taxes/subsidies). Similarly, in other agenda rules equal treatment with respect to taxes, subsidies or net transfers can be restricted to a certain percentage of the population or to a certain portion of the winning majority or losing minority.

We illustrate the working of particular agenda rules mentioned above in conjunction with majority rules in order to achieve second-best-outcomes by simple examples. We also discuss how constitutions might be designed to encompass the examples. In particular, we show how the possibility of amendments can improve the allocation of public projects and can eliminate excessive taxation. Finally, we indicate how the constitutional requirement of secret ballots will affect our results.

The chapter is organized as follows: In the next section, we outline the model and define the range of available treatment rules. In section 8.3, we derive the main results for different constellations of projects and sizes of the group benefiting from public projects. In section 8.4, we discuss optimal constitutions in all cases. We conclude with issues for further research.

8.2 Model and Treatment Rules

8.2.1 The Model

We consider a standard social choice problem of public project provision and financing. The first period is the constitutional period. In the constitutional period, a society of N risk-neutral members decides how public project provision and financing should be governed in future legislative periods. We assume that N is odd and large. Citizens are indexed by j or $k \in \{0, 1, \ldots, N\}$.

In the legislative period, each citizen is endowed with a taxable private consumption good, denoted by e. The community can produce a public project g. Let v_j denote the agent j's utility from the public project g measured in units of the consumption good. For simplicity of presentation, we assume that v_j can take two values, $v_j = V_h > 0$ and $v_j = V_l \leq 0$, so that the citizens can be divided into winners and losers. We assume that v_j is a private benefit that cannot be taxed.[2] The *ex ante* probability that a citizen belongs to the winning group in the legislative period, and hence receives V_h, is denoted by p. $V = pV_h + (1-p)V_l$ is the expected utility of an individual from

[2] If v_j were a monetary return it could be taxed in addition to e. The results would be unaffected by this modification.

the public project. By the law of large numbers, p equals the fraction of winners in each period, provided that N is sufficiently large, which we assume throughout this chapter. We denote the supply of the public project g by $g \in \{0, 1\}$. $g = 1$ stands for the provision of the public project. $g = 0$ denotes the status quo. We denote citizen j's subsidy by s_j and citizen j's tax payment by t_j. Taxes and subsidies are expressed in terms of the consumption good. Then, the utility of citizen j in the legislative period, denoted by U_j, is given by

$$U_j = e + g\, v_j - t_j + s_j. \tag{8.1}$$

We drop the index j in U_j whenever convenient. $\tau_j = s_j - t_j$ denotes the net transfer for individual j. Finally, we denote the expected utility of citizen j at the constitutional stage by EU_j.

Public projects and subsidies are financed by taxes. We assume that taxation is distortionary. Let $\lambda > 0$ denote the shadow cost of public funds. That is, taxation uses $(1+\lambda)$ of the consumption good in order to levy an amount of 1 for public projects or for transfers to citizens. We assume that the production cost of the public project per capita is given by $k > 0$. The budget constraint of the society in the legislative period is given by

$$\sum_{j=1}^{N} t_j = Nk(1+\lambda)g + (1+\lambda) \sum_{j=1}^{N} s_j. \tag{8.2}$$

It is socially efficient to produce the public project if and only if

$$V = p\, V_h + (1-p)V_l > k(1+\lambda). \tag{8.3}$$

Throughout this chapter, we assume that the maximum amount of resources that can be levied through taxation is sufficient to finance the public project:

$$e > k(1 + \lambda). \tag{8.4}$$

Moreover, we assume that $e > V_h$, and hence that the benefits from the public project do not exceed the income of the individuals. This assumption simplifies the exposition, since we do not need to always distinguish whether $e > V_h$ or $e < V_h$.

8.2.2 The Game

The sequence of events is summarized as follows:

Stage 1: In the constitutional period, the society unanimously decides upon the constitutional principles governing legislative decision making.

Stage 2: At the start of the legislative period, a public project emerges and each citizen j observes the realization of v_j.

Stage 3: A citizen is randomly determined to set the agenda. The agenda setter proposes a project/financing package (g, t_j, s_j).

Stage 4: The nation decides whether to accept or reject the proposal according to the constitutional decision rule.

Note that individuals know at the voting stage who will be taxed and who will receive subsidies if a proposal is accepted. The constitutional principles will be introduced in the next section. Given a constitution with a set of principles agreed unanimously upon in stage 1, we look at subgame perfect implementation in stages 2 to 4. Stage 1 will not be considered as part of the game. We simply assume that societies choose the set of constitutional rules which yield the highest expected utilities in a subgame perfect equilibrium over stages 2 to 4. We make the following assumption. Individuals in stage 4 do not choose weakly dominated voting strategies. This standard assumption allows us to eliminate weakly dominated voting strategies and voting equilibria will become unique. Moreover, this assumption will allow us to derive the expected utility from a constitution as the payoff of a unique subgame perfect equilibrium and thus will make the comparison of constitutions clear-cut. Moreover, to simplify the description, we assume two tie-breaking rules in case of indifferences. First, if an agenda setter is indifferent between proposing the public project and the status quo, he will propose the change. Second, an individual who is indifferent between a new proposal and the status quo will vote for a change.[3]

8.2.3 Constitutional Principles

At the constitutional stage, the society decides about the rules governing the legislative processes. We follow the incomplete contract setting and assume that it is impossible to write a complete state contingent public project supply plan at the constitutional stage. Future states cannot be described precisely and therefore constitutions can only specify non-contingent rules. Whether an individual is a winner or a loser of the project can be observed by other citizens at the legislative stage. For instance, if the project

[3] Without such a tie-breaking rule, we would face the standard problem that no equilibrium in pure strategies exists. This tie-breaking rule is simply made for expositional convenience.

is a new road, people observe that people close to the road will suffer because of noise and others will benefit because they have easier access to their work place. Following the insights from the incomplete contract literature, such observations, however, are not contractible and cannot be used in constitutional contracts and therefore not in constitutional rules. We assume open ballots; hence, individuals can be divided into the majority winners and minority losers, *ex post*. In order to avoid ambiguous terms we will distinguish between project winners (losers) and majority winners (losers).

Given the incomplete nature of constitutions, the question is which type of constitutional principles can be considered. The restrictions on feasible constitutions are based on the following twin principles. First, every constitution or constitutional principle must allow for equal voting and agenda rights as fundamental democratic principles. An immediate consequence is that every individual should have the same chance to determine the agenda. Furthermore, decision rules determining whether a change of the status is adopted can only depend on the number of votes for a change and not on the persons voting in favor or against the status quo. Second, the democratic principles cannot require more information from citizens than a proposal, and voting with the possibility of non-participation. Given these democratic constraints on constitutions we can think of the following set of constitutional principles:

P1: *Decision Rules*

- m–majority rules:

  If a proposal to change the status quo receives a majority of m percent of the citizens ($\frac{1}{2} \leq m \leq 1$), the proposal is adopted.

P2: *Constraint of Taxation or Subsidization*[4]

- Constraint of taxation to majority winners or losers (CTW, CTL, respectively):

  Only majority winners or losers can be taxed.

- Constraint of taxation to $\alpha\,(0 \leq \alpha \leq m)$ percent of individuals, belonging to the winning majority ($CTW(\alpha)$).
- Constraint of subsidization to majority winners or losers (CSW, CSL, respectively):

  Only majority winners or losers of the voting process can receive subsidies.

- Constraint of subsidization to $\beta\,(0 \leq \beta \leq 1 - m)$ percent of individuals, belonging to the losing minority $\left(CSL\,(\beta)\right)$.

P3: *Equal Treatment Rules for all Individuals*

- Equal treatment of individuals with respect to taxes (ETT):

  $t_j = t_k$ for all $k \neq j$.

- Equal treatment of individuals with respect to subsidies (ETS):

  $s_j = s_k$ for all $k \neq j$.

[4] We do not exhaust all conceivable cases in this description and focus on those rules which will be used in this chapter.

P4: *Equal Treatment Rules for Majority Winners and Majority Losers*

- Equal treatment of winners (ETW):

  For two members $j \neq k$ of the winning majority, the net transfers fulfill:

$$\tau_j = s_j - t_j = \tau_k = s_k - t_k$$

- Equal treatment of α $(0 \leq \alpha \leq m)$ percent of individuals of the population in the winning majority (ETW(α)):

  For α percent of individuals in the population in the winning majority, the net transfer of two members $j \neq k$ must fulfill:

$$\tau_j = s_j - t_j = \tau_k = s_k - t_k$$

- Equal treatment of losers (ETL):

  For any two members $j \neq k$ of the losing minority, the net transfer must fulfill:

$$\tau_j = s_j - t_j = \tau_k = s_k - t_k$$

- Equal treatment of β percent of all individuals in the losing minority (ETL (β)):

  For β percent of individuals in the losing minority, the net transfer of two members $j \neq k$ must fulfill:

$$\tau_j = s_j - t_j = \tau_k = s_k - t_k$$

P5: *Equal Agenda and Voting Rights (EAVR)*

- Equal agenda rights (EAR):

  Every individual has the same chance of being recognized as an agenda setter.

- Equal voting rights (EVR):

  Every individual has one vote.

While the principles $P1$ to $P5$ satisfy the democratic constraints, we will see later that these principles do not exhaust all treatment possibilities. A second-best constitution is a set of principles from $P1$ to $P5$ which yields higher expected utility in the subgame perfect implementation than any other constitution.[5] Since EAVR constitutes the basic principle of liberal democracies, we will assume that every constitution must contain EAVR.[6]

It is important to note that the violation of the constitution can occur at two stages. After stage 3, a proposal may violate some of the treatment rules. In this case, the proposal is unconstitutional and the status quo prevails. After stage 4 and voting, the principles $P2$ and $P4$ need to be checked. Whether or not $P2$ and $P4$ violate the constitution depends on the voting itself. For instance, suppose CTW and $g = 1$ has been adopted. If a taxed individual has voted no and is in the minority, CTW is violated. Again, if one constitutional principle is violated after stage 4, the status quo prevails. Since agenda setters can always benefit from making a proposal in agreement with the constitution, no agenda setter

[5] The term second-best is used here in a very loose sense since we only consider principles within the set $\{P1$ to $P5\}$. This chapter serves solely introductory purposes.

[6] EAVR can also be justified by narrow economic arguments, see Gersbach (2004c).

would ever propose a project/financing package that violates the constitution in equilibrium.

We next observe that it is generally impossible to implement a first–best constitution. Since it is not verifiable whether an individual is a project winner or a project loser, there is always a possibility that a loser can determine the agenda. He will never propose a socially desirable public project as long as he is not sufficiently compensated. Every compensation, however, creates distortionary losses and is therefore inefficient from an *ex ante* view.

8.2.4 Socially Efficient Solutions

Welfare is determined in stage 1. It is obvious that the socially optimal solution from such an *ex ante* point of view is given by $g = 1$ if expected benefits per capita are larger than per capita taxes. Moreover, the socially efficient tax scheme should only allow money to be raised for the financing of the public project, since any redistribution activities are waste from an *ex ante* point of view. The socially efficient tax schedule is indeterminate since citizens are risk neutral. For instance, a socially efficient scheme is $t = \frac{k(1+\lambda)}{p}$ for all project winners and $t = 0$ for all project losers as well as for every individual $s_j = 0$. In order to implement such a socially optimal solution, a complete social contract would be necessary. We summarize the first–best solution as follows.

Proposition 8.1
A first–best allocation is given by:

(i) If $V \geq k(1+\lambda)$ *then* $g = 1, \quad s_j = 0 \quad$ *for all* j,

$$t = \begin{cases} \frac{k(1+\lambda)}{p} & \textit{for project winners} \\ 0 & \textit{for project losers} \end{cases}$$

(ii) If $V < k(1+\lambda)$ *then* $g = 0, \quad t_j = s_j = 0 \quad$ *for all* j.

Expected utility from the public project for each individual is given by:

$$EU = g\big(V - k(1+\lambda)\big)$$

In the following we assume that private benefits of individuals are observable at the legislative stage, but are not verifiable and hence cannot be used in social contracts. As it is standard in the incomplete contracting literature, constitutions can only specify state independent rules as expressed in the constitutional principles $P1$ to $P5$.

8.3 Examples of Constitutions

We next illustrate the advantages and disadvantages of particular constitutions when no complete social contracts can be written and EAVR is a given constitutional principle. Due to EAVR, every citizen has the same chance of being recognized as an agenda setter. If a citizen, denoted by ag, is determined as the agenda setter, two cases can occur: either $v_{ag} = V_h$ or $v_{ag} = V_l$. In both cases, the agenda setter wants to create the smallest possible majority for an adoption or rejection of the public project combined with the most favorable tax/subsidy package for him. The constitutions should ensure that no agenda setter simply proposes a tax/subsidy package to redistribute income without proposing a socially efficient project. In the following we introduce particular constitutions as examples for simple and interesting combinations of agenda rules, agenda setting rules and decision rules.

8.3.1 Constitutions for Socially Efficient Projects

We first look at constitutions assuming that it is socially efficient to produce the public project from the perspective of the first-best allocation.

We begin by describing a constitution which ensures that only project winners are taxed, and that every agenda setter proposes $g = 1$.

Proposition 8.2

Suppose that $p > \frac{1}{2}$. *Moreover, suppose*

$$V = pV_h + (1-p)V_l > k(1+\lambda) \tag{8.5}$$

$$\frac{1}{2}V_h > k(1+\lambda) \tag{8.6}$$

Then, under the constitution

(i) simple majority rule ($\frac{1}{2}$–majority rule),

(ii) CTW (50%)

both project winners and project losers propose $g = 1$.
The expected utility for each individual is given by:

$$EU = V - k - \frac{\lambda(N-1)V_h}{2N(1+\lambda)}$$

The proof is given in the appendix. The point of proposition 8.2 is that, from behind a veil of ignorance, agents agree that only majority winners and at most half of the population can be taxed.

The condition $\frac{1}{2}V_h > k(1+\lambda)$ ensures that even a project loser is better off by proposing $g = 1$ and by taxing 50% of the population that are project winners. The excess revenues of taxation are channeled to the agenda setter as a subsidy. The agenda setter will not subsidy any project winner in his majority coalition. Due to CTW(50%) he cannot form a majority that would support a simple redistribution proposal. Note that a taxed project winner could make a proposal $g = 1$ unconstitutional by voting against $g = 1$. This would lead to the status quo which, however, does not improve the defecting project winner's utility. Therefore, no member of the winning majority has an incentive to switch. Moreover, because of CTW(50%), a project loser cannot make a proposal unconstitutional by voting strategically and supporting $g = 1$.

In the next proposition we consider an alternative constitution that avoids any subsidization and that will provide the appropriate comparison.

Proposition 8.3

Suppose $p > \frac{1}{2}$ and $V > k(1+\lambda)$. Then, there is a constitution with:

(i) $\frac{1}{2}$–majority rule

(ii) CTW

(iii) CSL (0%)

where the project winners propose $g = 1$ and project losers propose $g = 0$. No taxation for redistribution purposes occurs. Expected utility for each individual is given by:

$$EU = p\big(V - k(1+\lambda)\big)$$

Proof

Suppose that the agenda setter is a project winner. He cannot generate any subsidies for himself because $CSL\,(0\%)$ acts as a general ban on subsidies. But he benefits from the public project. Because of $p > \frac{1}{2}$, he can tax all project winners except himself by the uniform tax rate $t = (1+\lambda)\left(\frac{N}{pN-1}\right)k$. Since $V > k(1+\lambda)$ and $V_l \leq 0$ we have $V_h > \frac{k(1+\lambda)}{p}$. Hence, for sufficiently large N we have $V_h > t$ and therefore all project winners will support the proposal. Project losers vote no, but the proposal will be adopted. Suppose that a project loser determines the agenda. Because he cannot generate any subsidies for himself and loses from $g = 1$, he cannot do better than proposing $g = 0$ and $t = 0$ for all individuals. Therefore, since no subsidies are generated, expected utility is equal to $EU = p\big(V - k(1+\lambda)\big)$.

□

In the next step we compare the constitutions in the last two propositions. We obtain

Proposition 8.4

Suppose $p > \frac{1}{2}, V > k(1+\lambda)$ and $\frac{1}{2}V_h > k(1+\lambda)$.
Then the constitution $\left\{\frac{1}{2}\text{–majority rule, } CTW\ (50\%)\right\}$ is more advantageous than $\left\{\frac{1}{2}\text{–majority rule, } CTW, CSL\,(0\%)\right\}$ if and only if

$$V(1-p) > k\big(1 - p(1+\lambda)\big) + \frac{\lambda}{2(1+\lambda)}V_h$$

Proof

The comparison of the expected utilities under both conditions leads to the inequality in the proposition where we have used that $\frac{N-1}{2N}$ is approximately $\frac{1}{2}$ for sufficiently large N.

□

The more valuable the public project, the easier it will be to fulfill the condition in the last proposition for the constitution $\{\frac{1}{2}$–majority rule, $CTW\,(50\%)\}$, i.e., the larger V is relative to costs k and tax distortions λ.

The constitution $\{\frac{1}{2}$–majority rule, $CTW\,(50\%)\}$ is inefficient if the inequality (8.6) does not hold, but inequality (8.5) holds since losers or winners recognized as agenda setters will not propose socially desirable public projects because the tax revenues from half of the population is not sufficient to finance the project. A modified constitution can ensure that socially efficient projects are undertaken in this case.

Proposition 8.5

Suppose $p > \frac{1}{2}$. Moreover, suppose

$$V > k(1 + \lambda),$$

then a constitution exists that ensures that socially efficient projects are always undertaken:

(i) $\frac{1}{2}$ - majority rule,

(ii) CTW

Both project winners and project losers propose $g = 1$.

The proof is given in the appendix. The constitutional rules in proposition 8.5 allow a project loser to tax all project winners which, in turn, generates enough subsidies to compensate the agenda setter. Note that an agenda setter will tax all project winners in the same way to maximize his subsidies. Hence all project winners will support the proposal and the $\frac{1}{2}$–majority rule is equivalent to a p–majority rule. Whether or not the $\{\frac{1}{2}$–majority rule, $CTW\}$ constitution is advantageous depends again on the comparison with the constitution $\{\frac{1}{2}$–majority rule, $CTW, CSL\,(0\%)\}$. The comparison follows the same procedure as in proposition 8.4 and is omitted.

We next consider the case that the fraction of winners is smaller than one half and hence a winning majority must contain project losers besides the agenda setter. We obtain

Proposition 8.6
Suppose $p < \frac{1}{2}$. Moreover, suppose $\lambda \leq 1$ and

$$V > k(1 + \lambda)$$

Then, the constitution

(i) simple majority rule,

(ii) CTW,

ensures that both project winners and project losers propose $g = 1$.

The proof is given in the appendix. Note that in the case of $p < \frac{1}{2}$, a project loser has an incentive to propose $g = 1$ if he can tax all project winners by V_h, and tax revenues are sufficient to subsidy $(\frac{1}{2} - p)N$ losers and the agenda setter himself so that they support $g = 1$. This is ensured when the project is socially efficient.

Again, the comparison with the constitution $\{\frac{1}{2}$–majority rule, CTW, CSW (0%)$\}$ determines whether or not the constitution $\{\frac{1}{2}$–majority rule, $CTW\}$ is advantageous for the case $p < \frac{1}{2}$. This comparison for $p < \frac{1}{2}$ follows similar considerations as in proposition 8.4 and is therefore omitted.

8.3.2 The Curse of Equal Treatment

Proposition 8.2 and 8.6 show that it may be optimal to limit treatment clauses to subgroups of a society. If we were requiring equal treatment for all individuals, more inefficiencies would occur compared to the constitutions in the last sections.

This is shown in the following proposition.

Proposition 8.7
Suppose

$$V > k(1 + \lambda)$$

Then the constitution

(i) simple majority rule,

(ii) ETT,

(iii) ETS

can be inefficient.

Proof
The inefficiency of the constitution with ETT and ETS can arise from two sources. First, suppose that a project loser determines the agenda. Because he cannot generate subsidies without paying for it himself by a larger tax, a project loser will never propose

$g = 1$. Second, if $p < \frac{1}{2}$, a project winner who proposes the project must propose a uniform tax rate $t = k(1+\lambda)$. However, no project loser will ever support such a proposal, even if a project winner tried to generate subsidies. Because of ETS, we have $s_j = s$ for all j, which requires a tax rate $t = k(1+\lambda) + s(1+\lambda)$ for a certain subsidy level s. Hence, a majority of project losers rejects $g = 1$.

□

Proposition 8.7 illustrates the inefficiencies caused by rules that require equal treatment concerning taxes and subsidies for all individuals because socially valuable public projects cannot be implemented anymore.

8.3.3 Constitutions for Socially Inefficient Projects

The next question concerns the nature of constitutions when projects are socially inefficient. We obtain:

Proposition 8.8

Suppose that

$$V = pV_h + (1-p)V_l < k(1+\lambda) \tag{8.7}$$

Then, a first–best constitution exists with

(i) $\max\{\frac{pN+1}{N}, \frac{1}{2}\}$ *– majority rule,*

(ii) ETT,

(iii) ETS.

Both project winners and losers propose $g = 0$ *and* $t_j = s_j = 0$, *for all* j.

The proof is given in the appendix. Proposition 8.8 shows how equal treatment rules work together with super majority rules. They can eliminate any danger that inefficient public projects are proposed or produced or that simple redistribution proposals are implemented, because everybody must be treated equally with respect to taxes and subsidies.

8.4 Discussion

8.4.1 General Constitutions

The preceding analysis has highlighted how various constraints on permissible taxes and subsidies can be combined with political decision-making. However, the analysis raises several issues for practical methods of decision-making: general constitutions, amendments and secret ballots.

The constitutions we have presented are different for socially efficient and inefficient public projects and even different within the classes of efficient projects. Naturally, one would like to design a constitution which encompasses all possible cases. There are four possibilities to address this fundamental issue which we discuss in the following also with respect to potential applications.

First, one could try to design a meta constitution which contains a decision rule on how to decide among different constitutions when a specific public project has to be allocated. However, it is unclear at this stage how such a meta constitution should be designed and it is doubtful whether the public can be convinced of using courts that decide in which case which constitution should apply. Moreover, it remains doubtful whether courts possess the required information. Finally, the constitutions have to make general rules for different cases. Therefore, meta constitutions are unlikely to be helpful in decision-making processes.

Second, one could select a constitution among all feasible constitutions discussed in this chapter which minimizes utility losses. It would necessarily be second-best, given a flow of efficient and inefficient projects with varying sizes of project winners. A second-best constitution is defined as a set of constitutional principles that yield a higher expected utility in the subgame perfect equilibrium in stages 2 to 4 than any other combination of principles from $P1$ to $P5$. As illustrated in this chapter, second-best constitutions depend on the distribution of net welfare gains or losses from public projects and of the size of project winners (see Gersbach (2004b)). However, it is doubtful that sufficient knowledge about the distribution of future public projects is available in a society which makes this approach difficult to apply.

Third, we can try broaden the set of constitutional principles by incorporating new decision, agenda and agenda setter rules. This is the most promising approach and will be pursued in the following chapters.

Fourth, we can consider constitutions allowing for second proposals or amendments which are ubiquitous in political debates. With amendments it is possible to direct democratic decision-making towards desired allocation of a public project while excessive taxation can be eliminated.

8.4.2 Amendments

We consider the most simple case of introducing amendments. An amendment modifies stages 3 and 4 in the following way:

Stage 3: Two citizens a_1 and a_2 ($a_1 \neq a_2$) are randomly determined to set the agenda. The agenda setters sequentially propose project/financing packages (g^1, t_j^1, s_j^1) and (g^2, t_j^2, s_j^2).

Stage 4: The nation decides whether and which proposal to accept according to the constitutional decision rules.

The essential idea of such amendment rules is that other agenda setters have a chance to make counter proposals which limit the expropriation of minorities and can avoid that socially very inefficient projects are implemented. However, the amendment possibility should not eliminate socially efficient projects. How such a balance can be achieved is illustrated in the following proposition. In this proposition we use the refined treatment rule *ETTaxed* which means that all individuals who are taxed (i.e. for whom $t_j > 0$) must be treated equally with respect to taxation. *ETTaxed* implies that the tax rates for all taxed individuals must be identical. Otherwise the constitution is violated. The treatment rule *ETTaxed* only serves the purpose of ensuring uniqueness of equilibria.

In the proposition we also use the absolute majority rule. Under the absolute majority rule every agent can vote either for g^1 or for g^2 or can reject both proposals. A proposal is accepted if it receives 50% yes-votes of all votes. Otherwise the status quo prevails. Moreover, we restrict our analysis to $\lambda < 1$, which is plausible anyway. A complete analysis of equilibria with amendments is quite complex and we restrict our results to a simple illustration.

Proposition 8.9

Suppose that the following constitution holds

- *two proposals are made sequentially*
- *absolute majority rule*
- *CTW*
- *ETTaxed*

Then, there exist equilibria that implement the following allocations:[7]

(i) If $V > k(1+\lambda)$ $(p > \frac{1}{2}$ *or* $p < \frac{1}{2})$ *the project will be provided. In the case where* $p > \frac{1}{2}$ *no subsidies are provided and the allocation is first-best.*

(ii) If $V < k(1+\lambda)$ *and*

α.) *if* $p\,V_h < k(1+\lambda)$ *the project will not be undertaken. No subsidies are provided and the allocation is first-best.*

β.) *if* $p\,V_h > k(1+\lambda)$ *and*

a.) *if* $p > \frac{1}{2}$, *the project will be undertaken and no subsidies are provided;*

b.) *if* $p < \frac{1}{2}$ *and*

[7] In various cases uniqueness does not hold.

b1.) if $p\,V_h > k(1+\lambda) - (\frac{1}{2} - p)\,V_l(1+\lambda)$ *the project will be undertaken;*

b2.) if $p\,V_h < k(1+\lambda) - (\frac{1}{2} - p)\,V_l(1+\lambda)$ *the project will not be undertaken and no subsidies are provided. The allocation is first-best.*

The proof is given in Gersbach (2004b). Proposition 8.9 and the proof illustrate the advantages of amendments in conjunction with treatment and decision rules. First, subsidies and therefore excessive distortionary taxation can be reduced because agenda setters compete for proposals. Any proposal that involves subsidization of the agenda setter can and will be successfully countered by amendments, independently of whether agenda setters are losers or winners. Second, the socially desirable allocation of the project occurs in more cases than without amendment, i.e. when the constitution

$$\{\textit{two proposals, absolute majority rule, CTW, ETTaxed}\}$$

is used instead of

$$\{\textit{one proposal, simple majority rule, CTW, ETTaxed}\}$$

since in the former constitution project losers are forced to propose the project in order to avoid being taxed in the second proposal.

Allowing for one amendment in proposition 8.9, however, still yields overinvestment in public projects. While efficient projects are always undertaken, sometimes inefficient projects are undertaken as well. We will see in the next chapter that there is still considerable scope for improvements in democratic processes.

An important feature of the above constitution is that it is universally applicable as it does not depend anymore on project parameters. Therefore the constitution in this section is closer to applications in public policy, e.g. when an assembly decides about an infrastructure project, such as building a road or a bridge.

8.4.3 Secret Ballots

Many of the tax and subsidy schemes in this chapter require that voting is non-anonymous or even public since CTW requires that it must be checked which way a taxed individual has voted. Modern communication technologies such as the internet may allow to make constitutional checks on rules such as CTW without the revelation of individual voting behavior through verifications of personal identification numbers. But today the constitutional rules in this chapter would require that voting behavior of individuals must be public, at least before a constitutional court. Public voting is often the rule in legislatures, but not in mass voting or elections. Secret ballots are mandatory in mass elections because people in power could pressure individuals into voting in a particular way (see e.g. Schelling (1960)).

With secret ballots the efficiency enhancing rule CTW is not possible anymore while other treatment rules such as ETT or $ETTaxed$ are still feasible because their validity is independent of voting decisions. Moreover, the power of amendments in restricting excessive taxation to generate subsidies is still at work. Therefore the constitution {*two proposals, absolute majority rule,* ETT} may be a reasonable compromise for practical decision-making with secret ballots when a community decides on a public infrastructure project. However, as we will see in the next chapter there exist better constitutions.

8.5 Conclusions

Our examples have highlighted the impact of several treatment constraints on taxes and subsidies and on social welfare. We have also pointed out the useful role of amendments. Numerous further questions arise in the context of constitutional treatment rules which will be taken up in the next chapter when we consider new ideas as well as general constitutions.

8.6 Appendix

Proof of proposition 8.2

(A) Suppose that the agenda setter is a project winner. If he wants to implement $g = 1$, he must form a minimal coalition with the project winners in order to create a yes–majority. Since $p > \frac{1}{2}$ and CTW(50%) the agenda setter will propose $g = 1$ and

$$t = \begin{cases} V_h & \text{for } \dfrac{N-1}{2} \text{ project winners} \\ 0 & \text{for remaining individuals} \end{cases}$$

$$s = \begin{cases} s_{ag} & \text{for agenda setter} \\ 0 & \text{for all remaining individuals} \end{cases}$$

Note that at the voting stage, everybody knows how he is taxed or whether he receives subsidies. Thus, a project winner who is taxed can only avoid it by voting no and making the proposal unconstitutional which, however, does not improve his utility. The subsidy for the agenda setter is

$$\frac{N-1}{2} V_h (1+\lambda)^{-1} - k\,N,$$

which is positive by assumption for large N. Eliminating weakly dominated voting strategies, all project winners support the proposal and all project losers vote no. Since $p > \frac{1}{2}$, the proposal is adopted.

(B) Suppose that the agenda setter is a project loser. If he sets $g = 0$, he cannot generate any subsidies for himself. Any proposal with $g = 0$ to generate taxes would make all winners worse off because of CTW, and they would reject it. Since $p > \frac{1}{2}$, no majority coalition for positive taxation can be found.

If a loser proposes $g = 1$, he must form a minimal coalition with the project winners. Suppose that he takes $\frac{N-1}{2}$ project winners, which is the maximal size of a group he can tax. The maximal tax rate he can impose on this group of winners while they still support a project proposal is $t = V_h$. He can set $s_j = 0$ for all project winners. The payoff the agenda setter receives this way is given by:

$$V_l + s_{ag} = V_l - kN + \frac{N-1}{2} V_h (1+\lambda)^{-1}$$

Hence, the proposal $g = 1$ with the derived tax and subsidy plan is more profitable than $g = 0$ if $s_{ag} > -V_l$ which yields:

$$\frac{N-1}{2} V_h > (1+\lambda)(k\,N - V_l)$$

For sufficiently large N, this condition is equivalent to

$$\frac{1}{2}V_h > k(1+\lambda)$$

Note that a majority of $pN+1$ individuals support the proposal of the agenda setter in this case, while all project losers except the agenda setter reject it. However, no agent has an incentive to switch. A taxed project winner would make the proposal unconstitutional by voting no because of CTW, which does not improve his utility. The agenda setter also benefits from voting yes.

(C) Expected net transfers per capita (taxes minus subsidies) at the constitutional stage are given by:

$$\left\{\frac{N-1}{2N}V_h - \frac{1}{N}\left\{\frac{(N-1)V_h}{2(1+\lambda)} - k\,N\right\}\right\}$$
$$= k + \frac{\lambda(N-1)V_h}{2N(1+\lambda)}$$

Hence, expected utility for individuals at the constitutional stage is given by

$$EU = V - k - \frac{\lambda(N-1)V_h}{2N(1+\lambda)}$$

□

Proof of proposition 8.5

The proof is derived from considerations similar to the proof of proposition 8.2. A loser can tax all project winners because of CTW. Since $e > V_h$, he can receive tax revenues $Np \cdot V_h$ that exceed $Nk(1+\lambda)$ by at least $N(1-p)|V_l|$ because $V > k(1+\lambda)$. Those revenues $N(1-p)|V_l|$ can be channeled to the agenda setter. Therefore he gains subsidies $\frac{N(1-p)|V_l|}{1+\lambda}$ from $g = 1$ which is positive and larger than $|V_l|$ if $p < 1$ as assumed, and N sufficiently large. All project winners vote yes, while project losers reject the proposal. The proposal will be adopted. It is impossible to propose any tax/subsidy schedule and $g = 0$ that would be adopted by a $\frac{1}{2}$ – majority.

Finally, no individual has an incentive to vote strategically and to make proposals unconstitutional. Project winners do not lose from $g = 1$ and have no incentive to vote $g = 0$. Project losers have no possibility to make proposals unconstitutional since CTW does not require that taxes of majority winners are strictly positive and thus a yes–vote by a project loser is not unconstitutional.

□

Proof of proposition 8.6

Suppose the agenda setter is a project winner. He can propose

$$g = 1 \tag{8.8}$$

$$t = \begin{cases} V_h & \text{for other project winners} \\ 0 & \text{for remaining individuals} \end{cases} \tag{8.9}$$

$$s = \begin{cases} -V_l & \text{for } (\frac{1}{2} - p)N \text{ project losers} \\ s_{ag} & \text{for agenda setter} \\ 0 & \text{for others} \end{cases} \tag{8.10}$$

The agenda setter can channel the remaining subsidies to himself. Hence,

$$s_{ag} = (p\,N - 1)V_h(1 + \lambda)^{-1} + (\frac{1}{2} - p)N\,V_l - k\,N$$

Then, such a proposal will be supported by other project winners and $(\frac{1}{2} - p)N$ losers. Obviously, the agenda setter himself will support the proposal because he is a project winner, does not need to pay any taxes and $s_{ag} > 0$.

Suppose the agenda setter is a loser. As we will see the best proposal is

$$g = 1 \tag{8.11}$$

$$t = \begin{cases} V_h & \text{for all project winners} \\ 0 & \text{for others} \end{cases} \tag{8.12}$$

$$s = \begin{cases} -V_l & \text{for } (\frac{1}{2} - p)N \text{ project losers} \\ s_{ag} & \text{for the agenda setter} \\ 0 & \text{for others} \end{cases} \tag{8.13}$$

The proposal would be supported by all project winners and $(\frac{1}{2} - p)N$ project losers and hence by a majority. The agenda setter is better off if and only if $s_{ag} \geq -V_l$. $s_{ag} \geq -V_l$ is feasible if and only if

$$pN V_h (1 + \lambda)^{-1} + (\tfrac{1}{2} - p) N V_l - Nk \geq -V_l,$$

which for sufficiently large N implies

$$p V_h \geq k(1 + \lambda) - (\tfrac{1}{2} - p) V_l (1 + \lambda),$$

For $\lambda \leq 1$ a sufficient condition is $p V_h + (1 - p) V_l \geq k(1 + \lambda) + p V_l (1 + \lambda)$ which is implied by our assumption $V > k(1 + \lambda)$.

□

Proof of proposition 8.8

Since it is socially undesirable to provide the public project, the constitutional rules should lead project winners and losers to propose $g = 0$ and no taxes and subsidies. Because of *ETT* and

ETS, no agent will ever propose taxes in order to generate subsidies since net–transfer $\tau_j = \tau = \frac{t}{(1+\lambda)} - t < 0$ for every positive tax rate t.

Suppose that the agenda setter is a winner. If he wants to finance the project, he must propose a tax rate $t = k(1+\lambda)$. However, to form a majority in favor of the project he must obtain a vote from a project loser, since a majority requires at least $pN+1$ votes because we have a $\max\{\frac{pN+1}{pN}, \frac{1}{2}\}$–majority rule. But a project loser will never vote for a proposal that will lead to $g = 1$. Obviously, a project loser will never propose $g = 1$. Hence, the constitution implements a first–best allocation.

□

9. Flexible Majority Rules[1]

9.1 Introduction

The last chapter has illustrated that majority rules may often produce inefficient provision of public projects. For instance, a majority may support a public project although the minority's losses outweigh the benefits for the majority. From an *ex ante* perspective, the expected utility is negative, but the public project is provided nevertheless. In addition, majority voting can give rise to excessive redistribution activities with the majority simply expropriating the minority.

Democracies can also fail to provide socially efficient public projects since winners may constitute a small minority and compensating part of the losses in order to form a supporting majority may require large transfers. Financing such transfers through the tax system may involve distortions that outweigh the net benefits from the public project. Finally, when losers from public projects have the right to determine the agenda, they can block the provision of socially efficient public projects by creating proposals that simply redistribute income from the majority to the minority.

In the last chapter it has been shown that fixed majority rules and constitutional treatment rules with respect to taxes and sub-

[1] This chapter is based entirely on Erlenmaier and Gersbach (2001).

sidies can increase the efficiency of the democratic process. But inefficiencies remain; in this chapter we introduce flexible majority rules and other complementary constitutional rules to mitigate the remaining disadvantages of democracies in the provision of public projects.

Under flexible majority rules, the size of the majority required for the adoption of a proposal depends on the proposal itself, eg. on the share of taxed individuals. As an example suppose that the size of the majority is equal to the share of taxed people plus half of the share of non-taxed people. Then, if the share of taxed people is 60% of the society, the required majority is equal to 80% of the population. If the share of taxed people only amounts to 20% of the society, only 60% yes-voters are required for the adoption of the proposal. Therefore, if the individuals who are taxed correspond to the group of beneficiaries from the public project, the size of the majority required for a change of the status quo increases with the size of the project winners group.

We examine the same model as in the last chapter where risk neutral individuals decide at the constitutional stage under a veil of ignorance how public project provision and financing should be governed in the legislative period. Again, democratic constitutions are understood as the liberal democracy constraint on the set of all feasible mechanisms to collectively provide public projects. In this chapter, however, we design constitutions truly under a veil of ignorance, i.e., when little or nothing about project parameters is known. We show that at the constitutional stage, individuals unanimously agree to constitutional principles involving flexible majority rules and costly agenda setting. Our main conclusions are:

First, if nobody is affected negatively by the public project, the combination of the following constitutional principles constitutes a socially optimal constitution:

- Taxation constrained to majority winners
- Maximal taxation of the agenda setter, i.e. he has to pay the highest taxes
- A ban on subsidies
- Flexible majority rules

Second, if the utility from public projects can be negative for some agents, the following constitutional principles yield a first-best allocation in almost all cases:

- Taxation constrained to majority winners
- Maximal taxation of the agenda setter and costly agenda setting
- A ban on subsidies
- Flexible majority rules

Under both types of constitutions only the individuals with a high utility from the public project want to set the agenda. In order to lower their tax burden they tax other agents to the extent that they still support the proposal. Subsidization is banned which eliminates excessive tax distortions. In the case where some agents are affected negatively by the public project, the flexible majority rules require unanimous support if the public project is not socially valuable and a lower level of support if it is socially valuable. Flexible majority rules ensure that a winning majority for the project proposal can be obtained if and only if the public project is socially valuable.

While we explore flexible majority rules in the context of public project provision, the idea could have broader applications in a variety of other circumstances. For instance, it might be useful to make the size of the majority dependent on the importance of the issue, captured by the associated tax volume. Then, large reform proposals may require super majority rules whereas marginal changes are voted on by the simple majority rule. Another application would be to let the size of the majority depend on the tax differences across the population which would allow to pursue distributional objectives in a society.[2]

This chapter is related to the literature on constitutional design and to a large literature on optimal collective decision rules and to the majoritarian logic (see e.g. Buchanan (1998) and Mueller (1989)). May (1952) has shown that the simple majority rule satisfies a number of axioms founded in the enlightenment era (see Schofield (1972) for a discussion). Guttman (1998) finds that under plausible conditions about project data the simple majority rule is second-best in a binary decision context. Recently Koray (2000) has outlined a method for viewing social choice functions themselves as alternatives, so that one can ask whether a social choice function selects itself. He shows that given enough richness of preferences the only self-selective social choice functions are dictatorial.[3] In this chapter we suggest that flexible majority rules can implement first-best solutions and provide an efficient bridge

[2] Flexible majority rules can also be applied in a variety of other circumstances. E.g. Gersbach and Pachl (2004) have designed flexible majority rules for central banks.

[3] See also the self-stable voting rules of Barbera and Jackson (2000).

between the twin problems of democracy: overcoming vested interests and expropriation of minorities.

The constitutional rules in this chapter induce agenda setters to propose only socially efficient projects. This chapter is thus related to the recent literature on efficient information aggregation through voting.[4] However, none of the existing papers in the literature is concerned with the design of the constitutional rules for agenda setting and decisions to implement efficient allocations of public projects.

An important remark about our approach to design constitutional rules is in order. We consider mechanisms under the liberal democracy constraint.[5] Within this constraint we use a constructive procedure, i.e. we design rules in order to achieve first-best allocations under various scenarios of uncertainty. We have not yet found a direct method to characterize the set of feasible mechanisms. Such a characterization would be necessary in order to built a general theory of constitutional design. We think that as long as no general theory is available, the constructive approach taken here is a useful substitute, since we can find rules which implement first-best allocations.

---

[4] An important strand of literature has examined the validity of the Condorcet Jury Theorem which states that majority rule voting allows efficient information aggregation (Young and Levenglick (1978)). Austen-Smith and Banks (1996), Feddersen and Pesendorfer (1994), and Feddersen and Pesendorfer (1996) have shown that taking into account the possibility of strategic voting does allow to generalize and reinforce the informational efficiency of voting. Others have relaxed the independence assumption and allow for correlated voters and still obtain efficient information aggregation (Ladha (1992), Berg (1993) and Berend and Paroush (1998)). For a survey see Piketty (1999).

[5] Without the liberal principles constraint there are always mechanisms for implementing socially efficient public project provision in our context.

9.2 Model and Constitutional Rules

9.2.1 The Model

We consider again the standard social choice problem of public project provision and financing, now with a continuum of voters. In the constitutional period a society of risk-neutral members decides upon how public project provision and financing should be governed in the legislative period.

In the legislative period each citizen is endowed with some private consumption good whose density on the unit interval is e. The community can adopt a public project with per capita costs $k > 0$. Citizens are indexed by i or $j \in [0, 1]$. We denote the utility of agent j from the provision of the public project by v_j. For simplicity of presentation, we assume that v_j can take two values (expressed in terms of the consumption good), $v_j = V_h > 0$ if $j \in [0, p]$ (project winners) and $v_j = V_l < V_h$ if $j \in (p, 1]$ (project losers). In the constitutional period agents do not know whether they will be project winners or project losers in the legislative period, i.e. in the constitutional period for each citizen his location j in the unit interval is a uniformly distributed random variable. Moreover, we assume that those random variables are independent and hence, by the law of the large numbers, the fraction of project winners and project losers will be p and $(1-p)$ respectively.

Public projects must be financed by taxes. We assume that taxation is distortionary.[6] Let $\lambda > 0$ denote the shadow cost of public funds. Hence the overall per capita costs of the public project

[6] It is well known (e.g. Buchanan and Tullock (1965)) that without cost of redistribution the unanimity rule in this context is first-best.

amount to $(1+\lambda)k$ and we can represent the project data in a vector.

We denote by t_j and s_j the tax payment or subsidy of citizen j respectively and define the variable g that indicates whether the public project is provided ($g=1$) or not ($g=0$). Assuming that v_j is a private benefit that cannot be taxed,[7] the utility of citizen j in the legislative period is given by

$$e + gv_j - t_j + s_j.$$

Finally the budget constraint of the society in the legislative period is given by

$$\int_0^1 t_j \, dj = (1+\lambda)\left[gk + \int_0^1 s_j \, dj\right].$$

Throughout this chapter we assume that $e \geq V_h$.

9.2.2 Socially Efficient Solutions

The fact that citizens are risk neutral implies that it is socially efficient from an *ex ante* point of view to provide the public project if and only if

$$V := pV_h + (1-p)V_l > k(1+\lambda).$$

Moreover, as in chapter 8 money should only be raised to finance the public project. Any redistribution activities are waste from an *ex ante* point of view. A socially efficient tax scheme, for instance, is that a socially desirable public project is financed by project winners and no subsidies are paid. In order to implement such a

[7] If v_j is a monetary return it could be taxed in addition to e. The results would be unaffected by this modification.

solution, a complete social contract would be necessary. We summarize the first-best solution as follows.

First-Best-Solution

Any allocation where the public project is provided if and only if $V > k(1+\lambda)$ and where taxes are only raised to finance the public project is socially efficient (first-best) in an *ex ante* sense. An example for a first-best allocation is given by

(i) If $V > (1+\lambda)k$ then $g = 1$, $s_j = 0$ for all j and

$$t_j = \begin{cases} (1+\lambda)k/p & \text{for project winners} \\ 0 & \text{for project losers.} \end{cases}$$

(ii) If $V \leq (1+\lambda)k$ then $g = 0$ and $t_j = s_j = 0$ for all j.

In the following we assume that complete social contracts cannot be written. As it is common in the incomplete contracting literature, we assume that future states of nature cannot be described precisely and therefore a constitution can only specify rules for future social decision making. Given socially efficient allocations, it is important at this stage to summarize the sources of inefficiencies that may arise in legislative decision-making: There are four types of inefficiencies:

- inefficient projects are proposed and adopted
- efficient projects are proposed, but rejected
- efficient projects are not proposed
- inefficient redistribution proposals are adopted.

Implicitly, the second and third inefficiency mean that delay in undertaking public projects is costly. We adopt the extreme assumption that not adopting efficient projects results in utility from the status quo.

In this chapter we suggest new constitutional rules that - to our knowledge - are not yet implemented in any existing constitution. We will argue that these rules will improve the efficiency of public project provision.

9.2.3 The Game

We consider the duality of constitutional and legislative period as a substitute for the complete social contract that cannot be written. At the constitutional stage, the society decides about the rules governing the legislative processes. The sequence of events for a decision process in this context is summarized as follows:

Stage 1: In the constitutional period, the society decides unanimously about the constitutional principles governing legislative decision making.

Stage 2: At the start of the legislative period, citizens observe their location j on the unit interval and the location of all other agents. Citizens decide simultaneously whether to apply for agenda setting ($\psi_j = 1$) or not ($\psi_j = 0$).

Stage 3: Among all citizens that apply, one citizen a is determined randomly to set the agenda. The agenda setter proposes a project/financing package $\left(g, t_j, s_j\right)_{j\in[0,1]}$. Denote this choice by A_a.

Stage 4: Given A_a, citizens decide simultaneously whether to accept the proposal ($\delta_j(A_a) = 1$) or not ($\delta_j(A_a) = 0$).

Note that if nobody applies for agenda setting, the status quo will prevail. Moreover, individuals know at the voting stage who will be taxed and who will receive subsidies if a proposal is accepted. Given a constitution with a set of principles discussed in the next section, we look at subgame perfect implementations in stages 2 to 4. A comprehensive overview of implementation issues can be found in Moore (1992). An equilibrium for the subgame that consists of the stages 2 - 4 can be described as a set of strategies

$$\left\{\psi, A, \delta(\cdot)\right\},$$

where $\psi = (\psi_j)_{j\in[0,1]}$, $A = (A_a)_{a\in[0,1]}$, $\delta = (\delta_j)_{j\in[0,1]}$. Note that $\delta_j = \delta_j(A_a)$ depends on the proposed agenda A_a. For the voting game in stage 4 and for the decision about applying for agenda setting (stage 2) we will assume that

- **(EWS)** *Agents eliminate weakly dominated strategies.*

EWS is a standard assumption to eliminate the multiplicity of voting equilibria. Moreover, we denote the utility payoff of agent j in the legislative period by $U_j(A_a, \Delta_j, \delta_j)$. Obviously U_j depends on the agenda A_a which the agenda setter a has proposed, on the vote δ_j of agent j and on the votes of all other citizens denoted by $\Delta_j := (\delta_i)_{i\in[0,1];i\neq j}$. In order to simplify the exposition we assume that two tie-breaking rules are applied:

- **(T1)** *Suppose that agent a has proposed the agenda A_a. If $U_j(A_a, \Delta_j, 1) = U_j(A_a, \Delta_j, 0)$ for all possible votes Δ_j of the other agents, then agent j will vote against the proposal if his* *net benefit* $u_j = gv_j + s_j - t_j$ *from the proposal is smaller than zero and he will vote yes in all other cases.*

In order to formulate the second tie-breaking rule we assume that the voting subgame has a unique equilibrium.[8] In this case we can define the utility level $U_j(A_a)$ that an agent j will achieve if agent a has proposed the agenda A_a. Moreover, denoting the set of all possible agendas by $\mathcal{A}$, we obtain that an agent j cannot strictly improve his utility by setting the agenda if

$$\sup_{A_j \in \mathcal{A}} U_j(A_j) \leq \min\left\{e, \inf_{a \in [0,1],\, a \neq j,\, A_a \in \mathcal{A}} U_j(A_a)\right\}.$$

Under these circumstances we assume that he will not apply for agenda setting:

- **(T2)** *If an agent cannot strictly improve his utility by setting the agenda, he will not apply for agenda setting.*

In what follows we will - without referring explicitly to it - always assume that (EWS), (T1) and (T2) are applied. We are now ready to characterize the expected utility level a particular constitution can deliver. We say that a constitution denoted by $\mathcal{C}$ implements an expected utility U if, given agents have agreed on $\mathcal{C}$ in stage 1 the following holds:

If (EWS), (T1) and (T2) are applied, all possible subgame perfect equilibria under the constitution $\mathcal{C}$ yield a fixed expected utility U. Non-uniqueness of equilibria does only occur in out-of-equilibrium strategies or in the agenda setting stage.[9] A formalization of this implementation requirement is given in the appendix.

[8] We will show that for all constitutions that we will consider, (EWS) and (T1) imply that the voting subgame has a unique solution.

[9] Note that for all but one of the constitutions that we will propose, non-uniqueness only occurs in out-of-equilibrium strategies but not in the agenda setting stage.

Finally note that the constitutional rules are decided on in stage 1 by the unanimity rule. It is obvious that if a set of constitutional rules yields first-best, it will be approved unanimously in stage 1 since individuals are identical at this point.

9.2.4 Constitutional Principles

The rules in the constitution now have to specify:

1. Whether there is a special treatment of the agenda setter (**Agenda setter rules**).
2. Restrictions on the agendas that can be proposed (**Agenda rules**). An agenda consists of a project proposal and a financing package.
3. How the nation decides upon a proposal (**Decision rules**).

We assume open ballots. Therefore, individuals can be divided *ex post* into majority winners and the minority. Moreover we assume that individuals can observe whether other agents are project winners or losers. However, as in chapter 8 we assume that this observation is not contractible and hence not verifiable in a constitutional court. In order to avoid ambiguous language, we will distinguish between project winners (losers) and majority winners (losers).

Note again that we use a construction procedure and outline all rules which we found to be potentially of help to reach first-best. In order to formulate the rules that we will use in this chapter we need the following notation:

Notation

Let A_a be an arbitrary agenda. We denote the fraction of citizens that have to pay positive taxes by n_T. Furthermore we denote the maximal taxes that are proposed for a citizen by t^{max} and the total tax payments that are proposed in A_a by $T = \int_0^1 t_j \, dj$.

We will consider the following possibilities of designing constitutional rules:

Agenda setter rules

- *Costs of agenda setting [**CA**(a)]*
  The agenda setter pays a fixed amount of $a > 0$ if and only if his agenda does not lead to the provision of the public project.

Agenda rules

- *Maximal taxation of agenda setter [**MTA**]*
  The agenda setter pays the maximal tax rate that is proposed in his agenda.
- *No subsidies [**NS**]*
  The agenda setter is not allowed to propose any subsidies.
- *Constraint of taxation to majority winners [**CTW**]*
  Only majority winners can be taxed.
- The financing package must satisfy the budget constraint.

Decision rules

- *m-majority rule [**M**(m)]*
  If a proposal to change the status quo receives a majority of m percent of the citizens, the proposal is adopted.

- *Flexible majority rule* ***[FM(α, β)]***[10]

  This rule divides the population into the part P_T that - according to the proposal - pays positive taxes and the rest P_N of the population. A proposal is adopted if it receives an α-majority in P_T and a β-majority in P_N. $\alpha = \alpha(n_T, T, t^{max})$ and $\beta = \beta(n_T, T, t^{max})$ may depend on the fraction n_T of taxed people in the population, on the total taxes T and on the maximal tax rate t^{max} proposed in the agenda.

  The following special cases of the flexible majority rule are important for our discussion:

  - *Fixed participation rule:* $\alpha(\cdot) \equiv 1$ and $\beta(\cdot) \equiv \beta$ $(0 \leq \beta \leq 1)$.

  - *Threshold majority rule (fixed threshold)* ***[TMf(q)]***

    Under this rule β jumps from 1 to 0 when the share of taxed people reaches the threshold level q.

    $$\alpha(\cdot) \equiv 1 \text{ and } \beta(n_T) := \begin{cases} 1 \text{ if } n_T \leq q \\ 0 \text{ else.} \end{cases}$$

  - *Threshold majority rule (variable threshold)* ***[TMv(q)]***

    $$\alpha(\cdot) \equiv 1 \text{ and } \beta(n_T, T, t^{max}) := \begin{cases} 1 \text{ if } n_T \leq q(T, t^{max}) \\ 0 \text{ else.} \end{cases}$$

Note that the flexible majority rules [FM(α, β)] may depend on information generated by the proposal (n_T, t^{max}, T). Therefore, constitutions that use such rules produce a *feedback effect*: the actual rules governing the decision whether a proposal is consti-

[10] These rules are in fact flexible and double majority rules. The "double majority" feature will be discussed in detail in the next chapter and we solely use the term "flexible majority rules" throughout this chapter.

tutional depend on the proposal and hence in return the proposals that will be made will depend on those rules. In contrast, the rules [CA(a)] and [M(m)] do not depend on proposal information but may depend on project parameters. Finally [MTA], [NS] and [CTW] do not depend on any additional information. Note how the agenda and the majority rules work. If a proposal or the majority voting outcome violates one of the agenda rules or if it does not receive the required majority, then the status quo prevails. We will call a proposal A_a of an agent a constitutional if the triple $\left(a, A_a, \delta^*(A_a)\right)$ does not violate the constitutional rules. $\delta^*(A_a)$ denotes the equilibrium voting strategies if A_a is proposed.[11]

In the following sections, we will demonstrate that the agenda and decision rules introduced above are helpful to achieve optimal allocations. Note how flexible majority rules take into account how many individuals are taxed. For instance, under the fixed participation rule, the size of the majority increases with the share of taxed individuals in a society. If the individuals who are taxed correspond exactly to the project winners, the size of the majority required for a change of the status quo is increasing in the size of the project winners group.

9.3 First-Best Constitutions

In what follows we will - as noted above - assume that all entries of the project vector $\mathcal{P} = \left(p, V_h, V_l, (1+\lambda)k\right)$ are *observable* by all citizens in the legislative period. But they might nevertheless not be *verifiable* in front of a constitutional court. In the case where

[11] We show in the appendix that equilibrium voting strategies are unique for all the constitutions we will discuss.

some entries of $\mathcal{P}$ are verifiable by a constitutional court, constitutional rules can be formulated dependent on those parameters even if they are not known in the constitutional period. A court can determine them in the legislative period in order to fully specify the constitutional rules that will govern the decision about the actual proposal. Take e.g. the [CA(a)] rule and suppose that V_l is verifiable. Then [CA($-V_l$)] requires that a court determines V_l for the actual project under decision and sets the costs of agenda setting to $(-V_l)$.

An equivalent alternative view is that - instead of being verifiable in the *legislative period* - some parameters of $\mathcal{P}$ are known in the *constitutional period* and hence can be directly written into the constitution. In the following we describe our results in terms of the second view. Note that the more parameters in $\mathcal{P}$ are known at the constitutional stage, the more likely it is that one can find a constitution that implements the first-best solution and the less complex such a constitution will be. If e.g. all entries of $\mathcal{P}$ were known, a constitution could simply describe the first-best solution. First, however, we will state a special case where first-best is implementable, even if none of the parameters in $\mathcal{P}$ are known. After that we will present our results in a descending order of assumptions about which parameters are known at the constitutional stage.

9.3.1 No Negative Utility

In the first step we assume that $V_l \geq 0$ and hence nobody has negative utility from the provision of the public project. At the constitutional stage there is complete uncertainty about the parameters of the project. As we will see, a constitution with simple rules can ensure a socially optimal constitution in this case. We start with the most simple constitution, denoted by $\mathcal{C}_0(m)$ and given by

$$\mathcal{C}_0(m) := \Big\{ [\mathrm{M}(m)] \Big\}.$$

Without additional constitutional rules, however, the agenda setter will be able to fully tax a share $(1-m)$ of the population that he does not need to create the majority for his proposal. This leads to subsidization of the agenda setter and to the provision of socially inefficient public projects. We can avoid these inefficiencies by enlarging our basic constitution $\mathcal{C}_0(m)$ with the [MTA], [NS] and the [CTW] rule:

$$\mathcal{C}_1(m) := \Big\{ [\mathrm{MTA}], [\mathrm{NS}], [\mathrm{CTW}], [\mathrm{M}(m)] \Big\}.$$

Proposition 9.1
If $V_l \geq 0$ then the constitution $\mathcal{C}_1(m)$ is first-best for arbitrary m $(0 \leq m \leq 1)$.

Proof
In the appendix (see lemma 9.1) we prove that voting strategies are unique. It is shown that an agent j will vote yes for an agenda A_a if his net benefit $u_j = gv_j + s_j - t_j$ is nonnegative and no if it is negative.

We now investigate the agendas that will be proposed. Note that for all j: $\inf_{a \in [0,1],\, A_a \in \mathcal{A}} U_j(A_a) \geq e$ because of [CTW] .[12] Hence - according to (T2) - agents will only apply for agenda setting if

[12] This can be derived from the following reasoning: If A_a has been proposed by agent a then only the case where $u_j(A_a) < 0$ for some agent j is interesting. In this case agent j would reject the proposal. But since $V_l \geq 0$ such a proposal necessarily involves tax payments of j and therefore - according to [CTW] - the proposal is unconstitutional and the status quo prevails.

they can make a constitutional proposal involving $g = 1$ that will be adopted.[13] Consider such a proposal: Because of [MTA] and [NS], the agenda setter will try to propose an uniform tax rate in order to minimize his tax burden. [CTW] limits the possible tax rate for project losers[14] to V_l because otherwise, taxed project losers would reject the proposal. We distinguish three cases:

(i) $k(1+\lambda) \leq V_l$. In this case the agenda setter will propose $g = 1$ and a uniform tax rate equal to $k(1+\lambda)$ for all individuals and the proposal will be adopted since $u_j \geq 0$ for all voters. Hence $\psi_j = 0$ is a weakly dominated strategy for all citizens.[15]

(ii) $V_l < k(1+\lambda) < V$. Taxation for project losers is limited to V_l and hence project winners have to pay higher taxes in order to satisfy the budget constraint. Because of (T2) and [MTA] project losers will not apply for agenda setting. A project winner will propose

$$t = \begin{cases} \Big[(1+\lambda)k - (1-p)V_l\Big]/p & \text{for project winners} \\ V_l & \text{for project losers,} \end{cases}$$

which will be adopted since $u_j \geq 0$ for all voters. Therefore $\psi_j = 0$ is a weakly dominated strategy for project winners.

(iii) $V \leq (1+\lambda)k$. As argued under point (ii), in a constitutional proposal that proposes $g = 1$ and will be adopted, the tax rate for the agenda setter is at least $\Big[(1+\lambda)k - (1-p)V_l\Big]/p$ and hence his utility in $t = 1$ is not higher than

13 If he proposes $g = 0$, then [NS] ensures that he cannot subsidize himself without making the proposal unconstitutional. Hence the resulting utility is e.

14 Note that we call the part of the population with lower utility (V_l) project losers since they gain less than V_h.

15 Obviously, $\psi_j = 1$ never leads to a lower utility than $\psi_j = 0$. But, given that nobody else applies, $\psi_j = 1$ is strictly better than $\psi_j = 0$.

$$e + V_h - \Big[(1+\lambda)k - (1-p)V_l\Big]/p.$$

It is bounded from above by e because $V \leq (1+\lambda)k$. Hence by (T2) nobody would apply for agenda setting.

□

Proposition 9.1 shows that [MTA] and [CTW] deter project losers from setting the agenda in the case where their utility from the provision of the public project is low compared to the project costs. Project winners only want to propose $g = 1$ if it is socially efficient. Finally [NS] ensures that taxes are only used for project financing. Note that the [MTA] rule is not needed to obtain a first-best solution, but it ensures that the implemented allocation is always unique.

Note also that in proposition 9.1 we allow for a change of the status quo to be brought about by a share of yes votes that is smaller than 50% (i.e. by a minority). Since, however, the required size of yes votes for a change of the status quo does not matter, the possible constraint that majority rules must have $m \geq 1/2$ would not affect the result.

The result in proposition 9.1 can be easily extended to the case where we have an arbitrary number of nonnegative utility levels from the public project. Suppose that there are n ($n \geq 2$) different utility levels from the public project, ordered as $0 \leq V_1 < ... < V_n$. Denoting the fraction of the population with utility V_w by p_w ($w = 1, .., n$), we can characterize the first-best solution in the following way.

First-Best-Solution (Many utility levels)

(i) If $V := \sum_{w=1}^{n} p_w V_w > k(1+\lambda)$ then $g = 1$ and a citizen with utility level V_w has to pay taxes $t_w^* = \min\{V_w, \bar{t}\}$ $(w = 1, .., n)$ where

$$\bar{t} := \min\Big\{t \mid \sum_{w=1}^{n} \min\{V_w, t\} = (1+\lambda)k\Big\}$$

(ii) If $V \leq k(1+\lambda)$ nobody applies for agenda setting.

Proposition 9.2

If a public project generates no negative utilities then $C_1(m)$ is first-best for arbitrary m $(0 \leq m \leq 1)$.

The proof follows the lines of the previous proof. Note that only citizens with utility level $V > \bar{t}$ will apply for agenda setting and that because of [CTW] the tax rate for each citizen is limited by his utility level.

In the following, we derive optimal constitutions when V_l might be negative. In each section we introduce more uncertainty about the parameters of the public project.

9.3.2 Uncertainty Regarding *p*

In this and the following sections we consider the more general case where V_l is negative. In this case the fixed majority rule [M(m)] will either lead to subsidization of project losers (if $m > p$) or to proposals of project losers that are only made to avoid the provision of the public project.

If we assume that p is not known at the constitutional stage, we have to use a flexible majority rule in order to still achieve first best. To make the working of this rule more transparent we will use a slightly different representation of the rule for socially efficient public project provision:

$$g = 1 \text{ if and only if } p > p^* \text{ where}$$

$$p^* := \min\Big\{w \geq 0 \mid wV_h + (1-w)V_l \geq (1+\lambda)k\Big\}$$

and taxes are only raised to finance the public project.

Hence, for given utility levels V_h, V_l and for given project costs $(1+\lambda)k$, the fraction p^* is the smallest share of project winners so that it is still socially valuable to provide the public project. We define $a \vee b := \max\{a, b\}$ and

$$\mathcal{C}_2 := \left\{ \text{[CA}(-V_l \vee 0)\text{], [MTA], [NS], [CTW], [TMf } (p^*)\text{]} \right\}.$$

Proposition 9.3

Suppose that the utility levels V_h, V_l and the project costs $(1+\lambda)k$ are known at the constitutional stage but not p. Then the constitution $\mathcal{C}_2$ is first-best.

The proof is given in the appendix. Note that V_h, V_l and $(1+\lambda)k$ are needed to calculate p^* and therefore must be known at the constitutional stage or, equivalently, must be determined by a court at the legislative stage. Proposition 9.3 illustrates the power of flexible majority rules. If $p < p^*$ unanimous support for $g = 1$ is required since, according to [CTW] only a fraction p of the population can be taxed. Subsidization of losers is, however, excluded by [NS] and the public project will not be provided, in accordance to the socially efficient solution. If $p > p^*$ only the support of all taxed individuals is required for the adoption of

$g = 1$. Since $V > k(1+\lambda)$ and thus $V_h > k(1+\lambda)/p$, project winners will apply for agenda setting and will implement $g = 1$ with a tax rate $t = k(1+\lambda)/p$ for project winners. Note that we do not need to make any assumptions about the statistical distribution of p at the constitutional stage.

9.3.3 Uncertainty Regarding p and $(1+\lambda)k$

In this section we assume that only V_h and V_l are known at the constitutional stage but not p and $(1+\lambda)k$. Again we do not need to make any specific assumptions about the statistical distribution of p and $(1+\lambda)k$ at the constitutional stage. Since the threshold p^* now depends on the unknown parameter $(1+\lambda)k$ we have to change our majority rule from the previous section to a rule with a variable threshold:

$$\mathcal{C}_3 := \left\{ \text{[CA}(-V_l \vee 0)\text{], [MTA], [NS], [CTW], [TMv } (q^*)\text{]} \right\},$$

where $q^*(T) := \min\left\{ w \geq 0 \mid wV_h + (1-w)V_l \geq T \right\}$.

Proposition 9.4

Suppose that only the utility levels V_h and V_l are known at the constitutional stage. Then the constitution $\mathcal{C}_3$ is first-best.

The proof is given in the appendix. Note that the critical threshold q above which the yes votes of taxed individuals are sufficient for the adoption of the public project itself depends on the aggregate tax revenues generated by a specific proposal. Small aggregate tax revenues correspond with small costs for the public project provision. Therefore, the critical share $q^*(T)$ above which taxed individuals decide alone about the provision of the public project is smaller, since public projects are socially valuable for smaller winner group sizes as well.

9.3.4 Uncertainty Regarding p, V_h, and $(1+\lambda)k$

In this section we assume that only V_l is known at the constitutional stage but not p, V_h and $(1+\lambda)k$. Hence the threshold p^* now depends on the additional unknown parameter V_h. Therefore we have to adjust our majority rule from the previous section again:

$$\mathcal{C}_4 := \left\{ [\mathrm{CA}(-V_l \vee 0)], [\mathrm{NS}], [\mathrm{CTW}], [\mathrm{TMv}\ (q^*)] \right\},$$

where $q^*(T, t^{max}) := \min\left\{ w \geq 0 \mid wt^{max} + (1-w)V_l \geq T \right\}$.

Proposition 9.5
Suppose that only the utility level V_l is known at the constitutional stage. Then the constitution $\mathcal{C}_4$ is first-best.

The proof is given in the appendix. The flexible majority rule above is the most demanding since the critical size of q depends on the overall revenues and the maximal tax rate proposed by the agenda setter.

Note how $\mathcal{C}_4$ works: If the public project is socially efficient then the agenda setter can avoid the requirement of unanimous support by taxing a sufficiently high share of project winners and by imposing a sufficiently high maximal tax rate $t^{max} \leq V_h$. In this case the project will be adopted by the yes votes of all project winners. Note that an agenda setter will not propose an uniform tax rate $(1+\lambda)k/p$ for all project winners, since in this case $p < q^*$ and therefore $n_T \leq p < q^*$, which would imply that unanimous support for the proposal is required. Hence t^{max} has to be higher than $(1+\lambda)k/p$. Therefore, in order to avoid raising more overall taxes than are needed to finance the public project, the agenda setter has to create at least two groups of project winners: one with a tax rate t^{max} and one with a lower tax rate. If on the other hand $p \leq p^*$, then the agenda setter cannot avoid the requirement of unanimous support since by [CTW] the maximal tax rate t^{max} cannot be higher than V_h.

Note also that [MTA] in this context is not feasible since the incentives for project winners to apply for agenda setting would not be clear anymore: Given that nobody applies, a single project winner has an incentive to apply if the project is socially valuable. But, given that another project winner applies, it is better for him to stay back since not setting the agenda implies a positive probability to belong to the low taxed group while setting the agenda would always lead to the maximal tax rate.

Finally we note that for $V_l \geq 0$, the constitutions C_2, C_3 and C_4 implement a first-best solution. Hence C_4 implements a socially optimal mechanism for public project provision in all scenarios we have considered by now.

9.4 Conclusion

The flexible majority rules and the rules for agenda setting introduced in this chapter appear to be a mechanism to solve the allocation problems of democracies in the provision of public projects. We have shown that a constitution that implements a first-best solution can be constructed. This, however, requires that it is possible to divide the population in two groups (project winners and project losers) with the same utility level from the public project in each group and that the negative utility V_l of project losers is known at the constitutional stage. If this parameter is not known, there is a vote for judges to provide unbiased estimates of V_l in the legislative period. In other words, an unbiased estimate of negative externalities by courts is needed for social optimal public project provision.

Of course it would be more satisfying if V_l could also be endogenized in the decision via the agenda setting and voting process. We conjecture that this is not possible in the considered framework since in our opinion it seems impossible to determine $(1-p)V_l$ without requiring that the *whole* population has to vote for a proposal if it shall be adopted. But in this case subsidies would be necessary which would not be consistent with a first-best solution of the allocation problem.[16] If our conjecture is true, our results suggest a role for a constitutional court in the provision of public projects: Determination of negative utility from a public project in order to allow the efficient working of the flexible majority rule.

However, before the potential role of flexible majority rules in democracies can be fully assessed, a number of issues should be cleared by future research.

First, the rules [CA] (costly agenda setting) and [NS] (no subsidies) are constructed in order to deter the agenda setter from proposing high subsidies for himself and others by expropriating

[16] Note however that it is possible to circumvent this problem in a framework where there are fixed government expenses that also have to be financed by taxes and that are not subject to decision. In this case it would be possible to give "subsidies" to project losers via a cut of the taxes that have to be paid for the fixed expenses. If those expenses are large compared to the negative utility of project losers it is possible to compensate project losers completely by such tax cuts. In this case the unanimity rule is a first-best solution.

the minority. They also deter him from making unacceptable proposals in order to prevent the provision of a socially efficient public project. But of course, if interest groups are able to subsidize an agenda setter for making proposals in their sense, they can circumvent the intended effects of [CA] and [NS]. Hence, there have to be additional constitutional rules that prevent such subsidizations.

Second, it should be examined whether it is possible to modify the proposed constitutions in order to achieve first-best solutions when there are arbitrary many utility levels from public projects.[17] Moreover, it will be important to consider multiple public projects which may allow for efficient bundling (see e.g. Erlenmaier and Gersbach (2004)).

Third, will the possibility of amendments or second proposals at the legislative stage help to generate better outcomes? In our model such counterproposals are not necessary or even unwelcome since individuals that gain less from a proposal than others have the opportunity to wait for better proposals.[18]

Fourth, one could argue that flexible majority rules violate equal voting rights in a sense since the impact of a vote of taxed individuals can be different from that of a vote of non-taxed citizens. In our view it appears to be a matter of taste to restrict decision

[17] If there are more than one positive utility levels, then C_4 can lead to the provision of inefficient public projects since the decision rule will be based on the highest utility level.

[18] For constitution C_4 to produce first-best allocations for instance it might be necessary that the agenda setter taxes some project winners higher than others. If there is only one proposal at all, even the high taxed project winners will vote for the proposal since compared to the status quo they still achieve a higher utility level. However if they know that there will be further proposals on the same public project they would have an incentive to vote against the proposal, hoping that next time they will belong to the low taxed part of project winners.

rules to fixed majority rules. There seems to be, however, no prior reason to exclude flexible majority rules since the impact of votes on final outcome also differs under fixed majority rules.

Fifth, flexible majority rules require open ballots and are best suited for smaller communities. It appears to be possible however, that the new technologies through the internet allow anonymous identification of votes and persons even in mass voting and thus open ballots may be replaced by identification protocols (see also Walker and Akdeniz (1997)). Hence, implementation problems of flexible majority rules could be alleviated by the evolution of the internet.

While we have introduced flexible majority rules in the context of public project provision, the idea of flexible majority rules might have broader applications in democracies as we will discuss in subsequent chapters (see also Gersbach and Pachl (2004)).

9.5 Appendix

9.5.1 Formalization of the Implementation Requirement

In section 9.2.3, we have required that if (EWS), (T1) and (T2) are applied, all possible subgame perfect equilibria under the constitution $\mathcal{C}$ yield a fixed expected utility U and that non-uniqueness of equilibria does only occur in out-of-equilibrium strategies or in the agenda setting stage. A formalization of this implementation requirement is that the set of equilibrium strategies can be described by

$$\left\{\mathcal{E}(A^*) : A^* \in \mathcal{S}^*\right\},$$

where $\mathcal{E}(A^*) = \left(\psi^*, A^*, \delta^*\right)$ is a subgame perfect equilibrium and $\mathcal{S}^*$ is an arbitrary set of agenda setting strategies. Moreover, for each equilibrium agenda setting strategy $A^* \in \mathcal{S}^*$ the payoff

$$\bar{U}(A) = \int_0^1 1\{\psi_a^* = 1\} \int_0^1 U_j(A_a^*)\, dj\, da$$

expected in the constitutional period has to be equal to U.

Note that the fact that there might be more than one set of equilibrium strategies does not cause a coordination problem since the only possible ambiguity concerns a decision that involves only one person (the agenda setter) and hence there is no *strategic uncertainty*. We call a constitution *first-best* if it implements the expected utility $\bar{U}_{opt}$ that is induced by the socially efficient contract, namely

$$\bar{U}_{opt} = \begin{cases} e + V - (1+\lambda)k & \text{if } V - (1+\lambda)k > 0 \\ e & \text{else.} \end{cases}$$

In order to prove that the constitutions that we propose are first best, we show that

- Equilibrium applying and voting strategies are unique;
- If $V - (1+\lambda)k > 0$ then for all $A^* \in \mathcal{S}^*$ there exist $a \in [0,1]$ with $\psi_a^* = 1$ and for such a, A_a^* is an agenda that implements a socially efficient allocation;
- If $V - (1+\lambda)k \leq 0$ then nobody will apply for agenda setting, i.e. $\psi_j^* = 0$ for all j.

9.5.2 Proofs

In this section of the appendix we give the proofs for propositions 9.3 - 9.5 in the case where $V_l < 0$. If $V_l \geq 0$ the proofs are along the lines of the proof of proposition 9.1.

The following observations will be needed for all proofs:

Lemma 9.1

(i) Suppose that citizens have agreed on one of the constitutions C_1 - C_4 in stage 1. Then, given an agenda A_a, the voting strategies are unique, namely $\delta_j^*(A_a) = 1$ if the net benefit $u_j = gv_j + s_j - t_j$ from A_a is nonnegative and $\delta_j^*(A_a) = 0$ else.

(ii) Suppose that a constitution involves the principles [NS], [CTW] and [CA($-V_l \vee 0$)] and that $V_l < 0$. Then a project loser will never apply for agenda setting in equilibrium, i.e.: $\psi_j^* = 0$ for all $j \in (p, 1]$.

Proof

(i) For taxed citizens, voting no is strictly dominated by voting yes if their net benefit u_j is positive and vice versa if u_j is negative. For taxed agents with $u_j = 0$ or for non-taxed agents we have that $U_j(A_a, \Delta_j, 1) = U_j(A_a, \Delta_j, 0)$. Hence, applying the tie-breaking rule (T1) we find that citizen j votes yes if $u_j \geq 0$ and no else.

(ii) First of all note that because of [CTW] we have that the utility of a citizen j that does not apply for agenda setting is never smaller than $e + V_l$:[19]

[19] This can be derived from the following reasoning: Suppose that an agenda setter has proposed an agenda A_a. Only the case where $u_j < V_l$ for some agent j is interesting. But then $t_j > 0$ and hence agent j rejects the proposal (see lemma 9.1) implying that A_a is unconstitutional according to [CTW] and $U_j(A_a) = e$.

$$\inf_{a\in[0,1],\, A_a\in\mathcal{A}} U_j(A_a) \geq e + V_l.$$

If on the other hand a project loser a sets the agenda, we distinguish the following cases: First, his proposal A_a is either unconstitutional, will not be adopted or involves $g = 0$. Then, according to $[\mathrm{CA}(-V_l \vee 0)]$, the agenda setter will have to pay $(-V_l)$ and because of $[NS]$ will receive no subsidies implying that $U_a(A_a) \leq e + V_l$. But if on the other hand A_a involves $g = 1$ we again have $U_a(A_a) \leq e + V_l$ because of the negative utility and the ban on subsidies. Hence

$$\sup_{a\in(p,1],\, A_a\in\mathcal{A}} U_a(A_a) \leq \inf_{a\in[0,1],\, A_a\in\mathcal{A}} U_j(A_a)$$

for all $j \in (p, 1]$ and statement (ii) follows by the tie-breaking rule (T2).

We will now give a set of criteria that are sufficient to show that a constitution is first-best. In order to do so we note that for $a \in [0, p]$ the value $U_a(A_a)$ does not depend on a and define $U_W^{opt} := \max_{A_0\in\mathcal{A}} U_0(A_0)$ and

$$\mathcal{A}_W := \left\{A_0 \in \mathcal{A} \,|\, U_0(A_0) = U_W^{opt}\right\}.$$

□

Lemma 9.2
In order to prove that one of the constitutions C_1 - C_4 is first-best, it is sufficient to show that the following holds:

(i) If $V > (1 + \lambda)k$ then $U_W^{opt} > e$ and

$$U_W^{opt} \geq \sup_{a,j\in[0,p],\, A_a\in\mathcal{A}_W} U_j(A_a) \tag{9.1}$$

Moreover, all agendas in $\mathcal{A}_W$ propose a socially efficient allocation.

(ii) If $V \leq (1+\lambda)k$ then $U_W^{opt} \leq e$.

We denote these criteria by ***(SFBC)*** *(sufficient first-best condition).*

Proof

(i) First of all note that $\psi_j = 0$ is a weakly dominated strategy for project winners, since by equation (9.1), $\psi_j = 1$ never leads to a lower utility than $\psi_j = 0$, but, given that nobody applies, $\psi_j = 1$ is strictly better than $\psi_j = 0$ because $U_W^{opt} > e$. Together with lemma 9.1 we therefore find that applying and voting strategies are unique.

(ii) By [CTW] we know that $\inf_{a\in[0,p],\, A_a\in\mathcal{A}} U_j(A_a) \geq e$ and the tie-braking rule (T2) together with lemma 9.1 imply that nobody will apply for agenda setting: $\psi_j^* = 0$ for all j.

□

Proof of proposition 9.3

By lemma 9.2 it is sufficient to show that condition (SFBC) holds. Note that $U_W^{opt} > e$ can only be achieved by a constitutional agenda with $g = 1$ that will be adopted. Because of [CTW], we have $n_T \leq p$ for each constitutional proposal. Hence, if $p \leq p^*$, such a proposal will need unanimous support in the whole population. Therefore a constitutional proposal with $g = 1$ will not be adopted since project losers cannot be subsidized and would reject the proposal. Hence $U_W^{opt} \leq e$ if $p \leq p^*$. If on the other hand $p > p^*$, the best an agenda setter can do is to propose an uniform tax rate $(1+\lambda)k/p$ for all project winners since it minimizes his own tax burden and the majority needed for the adoption of the proposal. Since $n_T = p > p^*$ the proposal will be adopted if all project winners vote yes. But this will be the case since $p > p^*$ is equivalent to $V > (1+\lambda)k$ and hence the net benefit for project winners is positive. Therefore we know $U_W^{opt} > e$ and the corresponding agenda proposes a socially efficient allocation.

□

Proof of proposition 9.4

The proof follows the lines of the proof of proposition 9.3. Just note that in a constitutional proposal with $g = 1$ we necessarily have $T = (1+\lambda)k$.

□

Proof of proposition 9.5

By lemma 9.2 it is sufficient to show that condition (SFBC) holds. Note that $U_W^{opt} > e$ can only be achieved by a constitutional agenda with $g = 1$ that will be adopted. Consider such a proposal. [NS] implies that $T = (1+\lambda)k$ and because of [CTW] we have that $n_T \leq p$ and $t^{max} \leq V_h$. Hence

$$q^* \geq \min\Big\{ w \geq 0 \mid wV_h + (1-w)V_l \geq (1+\lambda)k \Big\} = p^*$$

and therefore if $p \leq p^*$, unanimous support for the proposal is required. But since project losers cannot be subsidized, they would reject this proposal. Hence $U_W^{opt} \leq e$ if $p \leq p^*$. If $p > p^*$ we show that the agenda setter can achieve the utility level $e + V_h$ by proposing an agenda of the following type: He taxes a fraction w of project winners by $t_{w1} := V_h$ and the other fraction $(1-w)$ has to pay for the rest of the project costs, i.e. their tax rate is

$$t_{w2} := \frac{(1+\lambda)k}{(1-w)p} - \frac{wV_h}{1-w}.$$

The fraction w has to be small enough in order to make sure that $t_{w2} > 0$. Hence, in this case $n_T = p$ and $t^{max} = V_h$ which implies that $q^* = p^* < n_T$ and therefore that the proposal only needs the unanimous support of the project winners. But since $t^{max} = V_h$, all project winners have a positive net benefit from the proposal and vote yes. Note that because of [NS] the agenda setter cannot achieve a higher utility level than $e + V_h$ and that all agendas that lead to the same utility level for the agenda setter necessarily involve $g = 1$, overall taxes $T = (1+\lambda)k$ and no subsidies,[20] which completes the proof.

□

[20] In order to avoid the requirement of unanimous support of the proposal in the whole population, the tax distribution among project winners has to satisfy:

$$n_T t^{max} + (1-n_T)V_l - (1+\lambda)k > 0.$$

10. Democratic Mechanisms

10.1 Introduction

The last chapter has illustrated that increasingly sophisticated agenda, agenda setter and decision rules yield an efficient provision of public projects in democracies, provided that agents observe who benefits and loses from public projects when the agenda is set. While this assumption is reasonable for a number of examples, such as the construction of roads, labor market reforms or the scale-down of the defense industry, it is not plausible in other circumstances. Consider, for instance, the increase of safety through a rise in the number of police officers in the street. There is no way that other citizens can observe who feels safer and who does not.

In this chapter we therefore discuss how democracies can be improved by constitutional principles when individual utilities are not observable by other people during legislation. As in previous chapters the constitutional principles assumed in this chapter must obey liberal democracy's fundamental principles of equal voting and agenda rights. Accordingly, democratic mechanisms are understood as the liberal-democracy constraint on the set of all available constitutions or mechanisms.

When an agenda setter cannot observe who benefits and who loses, the problem he faces is that he cannot impose taxes on the beneficiaries of a project only. Moreover, agenda setters do not know how high the proportion of project-winners actually is. Nevertheless, we illustrate in this chapter that democratic constitutions can achieve first-best allocations in many cases. The first important element in this chapter is that of majority rules requiring the adoption of proposals among both the set of taxed and among the set of non-taxed individuals. These majority rules are called double majority rules. The double majority rules act as a constraint on the taxes agenda setters will levy on other individuals. They can be combined with flexible majority rules where the size of the majority depends on the proposal.

The second important element in this chapter is that agenda costs are made dependent on whether a particular share of votes supporting an agenda under consideration is achieved or whether taxes are set above a critical level. By introducing such costs for agenda setting, individuals attempting to thwart socially efficient proposals by putting forward their own proposals can be deterred from agenda setting. In this context, the non-observability of other people's utility helps to steer appropriate agenda settings. It allows a society to set agenda costs at levels at which only project-winners will apply for agenda setting, whereas project-losers will not.

Our central conclusion is that the combination of the following rules yields efficient provision of public projects:

- flexible and double majority rules
- a ban on subsidies

- agenda costs where the agenda setter has to pay a certain amount of money if his proposal does not generate enough supporting votes or a socially desirable tax scheme

A second and more speculative insight is that a higher dimensional uncertainty about the project parameters – e.g. who benefits, how large the benefits are and how large the share of beneficiaries is – may make it possible to design rules under a veil of ignorance to achieve first-best allocations compared to cases when benefit levels are known *ex ante*. Higher dimensional uncertainty makes it possible to set agenda cost rules such that project-losers, who will not know how large the benefits are at the legislative stage, do not apply for agenda setting. Such a deterrence of project-losers from agenda setting is desirable since project-losers have an incentive to prevent the adoption of socially desirable projects by making unattractive proposals.

In this chapter we also illustrate that under dictatorial agenda setting and in the case when there are only project-winners, simpler constitutions can yield first-best allocations.

The chapter is organized as follows. In the next section, we provide detailed motivation for our approach. In section 10.3, we introduce the model and the constitutional rules. In the fourth section, we discuss first-best constitutions depending on the uncertainty about project parameters at the constitutional stage. In the fifth section, we discuss dictatorial agenda setting, the role of non-anonymous proposals and the case where there are only project-winners. In the last section, we summarize our conclusions and propose some avenues for further research. All of the somewhat elaborate proofs can be found in Gersbach (2002).

10.2 Motivation and Approach

There are several particular motivations and justifications for this chapter. First, we believe that we can provide a rationale why double majority rules are useful decision rules in practice. There are a variety of decision rules used in democracies with a double majority feature. For instance, in Switzerland and Australia two majorities are required to signify approval of certain laws: a majority of all electors voting and a majority of states. This is called double majority rule (see e.g. Saunders (2001)). Furthermore, many representative democracies have a bicameral Parliament and in most circumstances laws must be passed by both Houses. Since we are not examining a representative democracy or a hierarchy of federal and state levels, our double majority rules do not exactly match real-world examples. However, the reasons found in this chapter for using double majority rules to restrict taxation of minorities point in the same direction as the one pursued by framers of constitutions in Australia and Switzerland (see e.g. Saunders (2001) and Feld and Kirchgässner (1998) for a recent survey).

Second, our analysis is closely related to the fundamental issues in mechanism design. Two main results in the area of mechanism design represent polar cases for this chapter. First, in a mechanism design setting d'Aspremont and Gérard-Veret (1979) and Arrow (1979) show that the expected externality mechanism as a direct revelation mechanism is an *ex post* efficient social choice function implementable in Bayesian Nash equilibrium if agents' types are statistically independent, agents have quasilinear utility functions and they must participate in the mechanism. Second, the Myerson-Satterthwaite theorem (Myerson and Satterthwaite

(1983)) shows that there is no Bayesian incentive-compatible social choice function that is efficient *ex post* and where agents are free to opt out of the mechanism. The democratic mechanisms discussed in this chapter force people to participate and thus are not subject to the Myerson-Satterthwaite impossibility theorem. However, we restrict our analysis to democratic mechanisms where agents can apply for agenda setting and can only send yes/no messages (voting); therefore, the expected externality mechanism is not feasible. In short, from a mechanism design viewpoint it is unclear *a priori* whether we can reach efficiency or not because our problem is different from the models discussed in the literature.

A difficult issue arises in this context. Since we focus on democratic mechanisms, we cannot use the revelation principle to simplify the mechanism-design task as is usually done. The range of democratic mechanisms consists of all conceivable agenda setter rules, agenda and decision rules (which themselves are arbitrary functions of the project/finance package proposed by the agenda setter subject to feasibility constraints), and the liberal-democracy constraint. As will become obvious, such functions neither need nor ought to be continuous in all cases, e.g. when threshold majority rules are used. Therefore, even under the liberal-democracy constraint the range of possible mechanisms is extremely large.[1] Accordingly, we employ a constructive or inductive approach.

Our approach is constructive in the sense that we design rules which must fulfill the liberal-democracy constraint, but should allow a society to achieve first-best allocations under various sce-

[1] As long as we restrict all rules to piecewise continuous functions we obtain infinitely dimensional spaces comprehensively examined in Aliprantis and Border (2000).

narios of uncertainty. An alternative approach would be in a first step to characterize all feasible mechanisms and in a second step to prove the possibility or impossibility of first-best allocations. While a formal description is possible by making agenda setter rules, agenda and decision rules arbitrary functions of the proposal, it is not clear yet whether this approach allows for general characterization of democratic mechanisms. And this must be the long-term objective of the research on democratic mechanisms. Therefore, since we can design mechanisms with novel rules to achieve first-best allocations, the constructive approach appears to be a useful substitute.

A third motivation for our approach is the interest in new agenda setter rules. As far as we know, flexible agenda costs, where costs depend on the share of supporting votes and on the requirement that agenda setters must pay the highest tax they are proposing, are new rules that might be helpful in democratic decision-making.

This chapter is again a study in constructive constitutional economics. It is open whether the complexity of the rules proposed in the chapter may exceed those a society wants to incur.[2] Nonetheless the idea of using flexible and double majority rules and making agenda costs dependent on the share of supporting votes could be relevant for institutional designs in democracies.

The constitutional rules in this chapter induce agenda setters to propose only socially efficient projects. The chapter is thus related to the recent literature on efficient information aggregation through voting.

[2] There has been an important discussion on how simplicity of rules (e.g. Epstein (1995)) can guide the selection of rules.

However, none of the existing papers in the literature is concerned with the design of constitutional rules for agenda setting and decisions to implement efficient allocations of public projects.

10.3 Model and Treatment Rules

10.3.1 The Model

We consider again the standard social choice problem of public project provision and financing introduced in the last chapter and repeated here for completeness. In the constitutional period a society of risk-neutral members decides how public project provision and financing should be governed in the legislative period. Citizens are indexed by $j \in [0, 1]$.

In the legislative period each citizen is endowed with e units of a private consumption good. The community can adopt a public project with per capita costs $k > 0$. Let v_j denote the utility of agent j from the provision of the public project. Seen from the constitutional period the utility v_j is unknown and hence can be interpreted as a random variable. For simplicity of presentation, we assume that v_j can take two values (expressed in terms of the consumption good), $v_j = V_h > 0$ (project-winners) and $v_j = V_l < V_h$ (project-losers) with probability p and $(1 - p)$ respectively. Throughout this chapter we assume that $V_l < 0$ and that project-losers indeed are harmed by the public project. We comment in the final section on the way in which our results are affected by assuming $V_l > 0$. We further assume that the realization of the utility is stochastically independent across agents.

Hence, by the law of large numbers, p equals the fraction of winners in each period.

Public projects must be financed by taxes. We assume that taxation is distortionary. Let $\lambda > 0$ denote the shadow cost of public funds. Hence the overall per capita costs of the public project amount to $(1+\lambda)k$ and we can represent the project data with a vector $\mathcal{P} = \big(p, V_h, V_l, (1+\lambda)k\big)$.

We use t_j and s_j to denote a citizen $j's$ tax payment or subsidy, respectively. We define the variable g as indicating whether the public project is provided ($g = 1$) or not ($g = 0$). Assuming that v_j is a private benefit that cannot be taxed, the utility U_j of citizen j in the legislative period is given by

$$U_j = e + gv_j - t_j + s_j.$$

We drop the index j in U_j whenever convenient. Finally, the budget constraint of the society in the legislative period is given by

$$\int_0^1 t_j \, dj = (1+\lambda)\left[gk + \int_0^1 s_j \, dj\right]$$

We assume throughout the chapter that e is sufficiently larger than V_h, so that individuals can be taxed at a rate that is at least equal to the maximal benefits they may receive from the public project.

10.3.2 Socially Efficient Solutions

The fact that citizens are risk-neutral implies that, from an *ex ante* point of view, it is socially efficient to provide the public project if and only if

$$V := pV_h + (1-p)V_l > k(1+\lambda)$$

and taxes are raised solely to finance the public project. Any redistribution activities are detrimental from an *ex ante* point of view. A socially efficient tax scheme, for instance, is one where a socially desirable public project is financed by project-winners and no subsidies are paid. In order to implement such a solution, a complete social contract would be necessary. We summarize our observation as follows.

First-Best Allocation:

Any allocation that provides the public project if and only if $V > k(1+\lambda)$ *and that raises taxes only to finance the public project is socially efficient.*

An example for a first–best allocation is given by:

(i) If $V > k(1+\lambda)$ then $g = 1$,

$$t = \begin{cases} k(1+\lambda)/p & \text{for project-winners} \\ 0 & \text{for project-losers} \end{cases}$$

$s_j = 0$ for all j.

(ii) If $V \leq k(1+\lambda)$ then $g = 0$ and $t_j = s_j = 0$ for all j.

As in the previous chapters, we remain in the incomplete contract framework. Moreover, in this chapter we assume that individual utility levels cannot be observed by other persons. In particular, an agenda setter faces the problem that he cannot impose taxation on project-winners only, because all persons are alike from his perspective. As discussed in more detail in section 10.5, democratic mechanisms become more complex especially because of the third source of inefficiency. Democratic mechanisms must ensure that project-losers cannot set the agenda and block the adoption of efficient projects. Also in section 10.5, we illustrate by an example that much simpler mechanisms would solve the fourth and the first two inefficiencies but not the third one.

10.3.3 The Game

We consider the duality of constitutional and legislative periods as a substitute for the complete social contract, which cannot be written. At the constitutional stage, the society decides about the rules governing the legislative processes. The sequence of events for a decision process in this context is summarized as follows:

Stage 1: In the constitutional period, the society decides unanimously about the constitutional principles governing legislative decision-making.

Stage 2: At the start of the legislative period, citizens observe their own utility v_j. Citizens decide simultaneously whether to apply for agenda setting ($\psi_j = 1$) or not ($\psi_j = 0$).

Stage 3: Among all citizens that apply, one citizen a is determined randomly to set the agenda. The agenda setter proposes a project/financing package $(g, t_j, s_j)_{j\in[0,1]}$. Denote this choice by A_a.

Stage 4: Given A_a, citizens decide simultaneously whether to accept the proposal ($\delta_j(A_a) = 1$) or not ($\delta_j(A_a) = 0$).

Note that if nobody applies for agenda setting, the status quo will prevail. Moreover, individuals know at the voting stage who will be taxed and who will receive subsidies if the proposal is accepted. Obviously, the status quo also prevails if a proposal to change it does not receive enough yes–votes as required by the majority voting rule. Given a constitution with a set of principles discussed in the next section, we look at implementations in stages 2 to 4. An equilibrium for the stages 2 to 4 can be described as a set of strategies

$$\{\psi, A, \delta(\cdot)\}$$

where $\psi = (\psi_j)_{j\in[0,1]}$, $A = (A_a)_{a\in[0,1]}$, $\delta = (\delta_j)_{j\in[0,1]}$ and $\delta_j = \delta_j(A_a)$ depend on the proposed agenda A_a. To derive an equilibrium, we will use weak dominance criteria as in chapter 9.[3] For the voting game in stage 4 and for the decision about applying for agenda setting (stage 2) we will assume that

- **(EWS)** *Agents eliminate weakly dominated strategies.*

In order to apply the dominance solution concept in all circumstances at the agenda setting stage, two additional variants of weak dominance are used to obtain uniqueness. First, weak dominance for agenda application strategies is used, given uniqueness of voting equilibria and hence elimination of weakly dominant voting strategies. Second, if needed, we apply iterated weak dominance. The latter is required in situations as in proposition 10.1,

[3] Since there is incomplete information about the utilities from the project, given a specific *a priori* distribution, the dominance solution concept also yields perfect Bayesian Nash equilibria.

where not applying for agenda setting is weakly dominated only for project-winners. If, however, project-winners apply for agenda setting and non-application by project-winners is eliminated, it will be weakly dominant for project-losers also to apply. All types of the weak dominance concept (see e.g. also Fudenberg and Tirole (1992)) are assumed to be incorporated in (EWS).

We use $U_j(A_a, \Delta_j, \delta_j)$ to denote the utility payoff of agent j given that an agenda A_a is proposed by a and given the votes $\Delta_j = (\delta_i)_{i \in [0,1]; i \neq j}$ of all other citizens and his own vote (δ_j). In order to simplify the exposition, we assume that the following three tie-breaking rules are applied. (T1) and (T2) are the same as in chapter 9.

To simplify the exposition, we use in addition:

- ***(T3)*** *If an agenda setter is indifferent as to an agenda which leads to $g = 1$ and another which yields $g = 0$, he will propose the former.*

We assume again that the voting subgame has a unique equilibrium[4] and continue to use $U_j(A_a)$ to define the utility level that an agent j will achieve if agent a has proposed the agenda A_a and $\mathcal{A}$ for the set of all possible agendas. Note that $U_j(A_j)$ includes the optimal voting strategies of all agents and that of agent j in particular. In what follows we will always assume - without referring to the fact explicitly - that (EWS), (T1), (T2) and (T3) are applied. We are now in a position to characterize the expected utility level that a particular constitution can deliver. We can say that a constitution, denoted by CO, implements an expected util-

[4] It is straightforward to show that (EWS) and (T1) imply a unique solution for the voting subgame for all constitutions under consideration.

ity U if, given agents have agreed on CO in stage 1, the following holds: If (EWS), (T1), (T2) and (T3) are applied, all possible equilibria under the constitution CO yield the expected utility U. Non-uniqueness of equilibria can occur in the agenda setting stage with respect to who applies for agenda setting and to the distribution of taxes.

We call a constitution *first-best* if it implements the expected utility $\bar{U}_{opt}$ induced by the socially efficient contract, namely

$$\bar{U}_{opt} = \begin{cases} e + V - (1+\lambda)k & \text{if } V - (1+\lambda)k > 0 \\ e & \text{else} \end{cases}$$

Since individuals are identical at the constitutional stage, we can apply the unanimity rule for the society's decision about the constitutional rules.

A constitution that implements the first-best solution must be associated with unique applying and voting strategies and proposals of $g = 1$ if and only if the project is efficient. However, it is not necessary for the financing proposal to be unique with respect to the distribution of taxes (for details see Gersbach (2002)).

10.3.4 Constitutional Principles

We assume that in the legislative stage individuals cannot observe whether other individuals benefit or lose from the public project. They only observe their own utility gain or loss. The rules in the constitution now have to specify:

1. whether there is a special treatment of the agenda setter (**agenda setter rules**).

2. which restrictions on the agendas are imposed, i.e. definition of all constitutional agendas (**agenda rules**). An agenda consists of a project proposal and a financing package.
3. how the nation decides about a proposal (**decision rules**).

In order to formulate the constitutional rules we introduce the following notation:

Notation

Let A be an arbitrary agenda. We use n_T to denote the fraction of citizens that have to pay positive taxes. We use r to denote the share of yes–votes for a proposal to change the status quo. By analogy, r_T and r_{NT} denote the share of yes–votes for a proposal among the set of taxed and non-taxed individuals respectively. Furthermore, we use $\bar{t}$ to denote the average tax rate proposed among the set of taxed people and $T = \int_0^1 t_j \, dj$ to denote the total tax payments proposed in A. Finally, we use $t^{\min}$ to denote the minimal tax rate of an agenda A.

Hence, we have

$$\bar{t} := \frac{\int\limits_0^1 t_j d_j}{\int\limits_0^1 1\{t_j > 0\} dj}, \qquad t^{\min} = \min_{t_j > 0}\{t_j\},$$

where $1\{t_j > 0\}$ is the indicator function. Since the set of feasible rules under the liberal-democracy constraint is still very large, we follow again a constructive approach. We will need the following possibilities of designing constitutional rules:

Agenda Setter Rules

- *Costs of agenda setting* ***[CA(b)]***

  The agenda setter has to pay a fixed amount of $b > 0$ if his agenda does not lead to the provision of the public project.

- *Flexible costs of agenda setting* ***[CA*** $(b_1, b_2(r))$***]***

  The agenda setter has to pay a fixed amount of $b_1 \geq 0$ if his agenda does not lead to the provision of the public project. Additionally, he pays $b_2(r)$ if the share of supporting votes is smaller than $r\,(0 \leq r \leq 1)$. Clearly, $CA(b_1, 0)$ corresponds to fixed costs of agenda setting.

Agenda Rules

- *No subsidies* ***[NS]***

  The agenda setter is not allowed to propose any subsidies.

- The financing package must satisfy the budget constraint.

Decision Rules

- *m-majority rule* ***[M(m)]***

  If a proposal to change the status quo receives a majority of m percent of the citizens, the proposal is adopted.

- *Flexible majority rule*

  This rule divides the population into the part P_T that - according to the proposal - has to pay positive taxes $(t_j > 0)$ and the remaining population P_N. A proposal is adopted if it receives an m percent majority of the citizens, where $m(n_T, T, \bar{t})$ may depend on the fraction n_T of taxed people in the population, on the total taxes T and on the average tax rate $\bar{t}$ proposed in the agenda.

The following special cases of the flexible majority rule are important for our discussion:

- Threshold majority rule (fixed threshold)
  [**TMf** $(m_1(n_T \leq q), m_2)$].
  Under this rule m jumps from m_1 to m_2 when the proportion of taxed people reaches the threshold level q, i.e.

$$m = \begin{cases} m_1 & \text{if} \quad n_T \leq q \\ m_2 & \text{else} \end{cases}$$

- Threshold majority rule (variable threshold)
  [**TMv** $(m_1(n_1 \leq q), m_2)$]

$$m = \begin{cases} m_1 & \text{if} \quad n_T \leq q(T, \bar{t}, t^{\min}) \\ m_2 & \text{else} \end{cases}$$

- *Double majority rule*

Under this rule, a proposal is only accepted if it is adopted among the set of taxed individuals and among the set of non-taxed individuals. The pure case of double majority rules is given by:

- Fixed double majority rule m [**DM**(m)].
  A proposal is adopted if $r_T \geq m$ and $r_{NT} \geq m$.

Double majority rules can be combined with flexible majority rules. For instance:

- Threshold double majority rule [**DTMf**$(m_1(n_T \leq q), m_2))$].
  Under this rule m jumps from m_1 to m_2 when the pro-

portion of taxed people reaches the threshold level q. A proposal is accepted if $r_T \geq m$ and $r_{NT} \geq m$.

Double majority rules require that the shares of yes–votes among taxed individuals and among non-taxed individuals are sufficient in themselves to adopt the project. A weaker requirement is that the share of yes–votes among the taxed population must be at least equal to the share of yes–votes in the non-taxed part of the population. The conclusions in this chapter do not depend on which concept of majority rules is used.

Note that both majority rules and [CA (b)] may depend on information generated by the proposal $(n_T, \bar{t}, T, t^{\min})$. Moreover, note that the constitutionality check occurs both at the proposal and at the voting stage. If a proposal or the majority voting outcome violates one of the agenda or decision rules, then the status quo prevails, since the constitution is violated and the proposal is void. This implies that the constitutional check on proposals may only be possible after votes have been cast.

10.4 First-Best Constitutions

Our major assumption is that at the legislative stage individuals cannot observe whether other individuals are project winners or losers. The remaining question is as in the previous chapter which entries of the project vector $\mathcal{P} = \big(p, V_h, V_l, (1+\lambda)k\big)$ are *verifiable* in front of a constitutional court in the legislative period. When some entries of $\mathcal{P}$ are verifiable in a constitutional court, constitutional rules can be formulated dependent on those parameters even if they are not known in the constitutional period, since a court can determine them in the legislative period.

An equivalent alternative view is that instead of being verifiable in the *legislative period* some parameters of $\mathcal{P}$ are known in the *constitutional period* and hence can be written into the constitution directly. In the following, we describe our results in terms of the second view.

Note that the greater the number of parameters in $\mathcal{P}$ known at the constitutional stage, the more likely it is that one can find a constitution that implements the first-best solution and the less complex such a constitution will be. Therefore, we will present our results in a descending order of assumptions about the parameters known at the constitutional stage. This exposition will show that the complexity of optimal constitutional rules increases as more parameters at the constitutional stage are considered uncertain.

10.4.1 Uncertainty About Winners and Losers

We begin with the simplest case where all elements of $\mathcal{P} = (p, V_h, V_l, (1+\lambda)k)$ are known at the constitutional stage while there is uncertainty for the individuals whether they will be project winners or losers. And note that an agenda setter cannot observe whether other individuals are project winners or losers. We obtain:

Proposition 10.1

Suppose that all elements of $\mathcal{P} = (V_h, V_l, p, (1+\lambda)k)$ *are known at the constitutional stage.*

(i) If $V \geq k(1+\lambda)$*, the constitution*

$CO_1 := \{[CA(-V_l)], [NS], [M(p)]\}$ *is first-best.*

(ii) If $V < k(1+\lambda)$, the constitution
$CO_2 := \{[CA(-V_l)], [NS], [M(1)]\}$ *is first-best.*

The proof of proposition 10.1 as well as all other proofs are given in Gersbach (2002). Proposition 10.1 shows that there is no problem in achieving a first-best allocation if project data are known at the constitutional stage even if the agenda setter does not know who benefits from the public project. Consider case (i). An agenda setter can tax all other individuals by $t = (1+\lambda)k$. Since $V_h > V > k(1+\lambda)$, the proposal ($g = 1, t_j = (1+\lambda)k$ for all j, $j \neq a$, $t_a = 0$, $s_j = 0$ for all j) will be supported by all project-winners and therefore receives a $p-$majority as required for adoption. Since an agenda setter can always propose zero taxes for himself, his utility is either $e + V_l$ (if project-loser) or $e + V_h$ (if project-winner) if he proposes $g = 1$ with the above financing scheme. Therefore, applying for agenda setting is a weakly dominant strategy for project-winners.

If an individual does not apply for agenda setting, he risks paying taxes if others apply for agenda setting. Moreover, because of $[NS]$ he will never receive subsidies. Therefore, project-losers also apply for agenda setting under the constitution CO_1 and propose $g = 1$ because of agenda setting costs.

The second part follows from the observation that project-losers never support a proposal $g = 1$ since they cannot receive subsidies. Therefore no agenda setter can form a majority for $g = 1$. Thus, no agent applies for agenda setting because of agenda setting costs and the status quo prevails.

In the next section we search for optimal constitutions when there is uncertainty in the constitutional period whether projects are efficient or not.

10.4.2 Uncertainty Regarding V_h

We assume in this section that there is uncertainty in the constitutional period about the size of the utility gain V_h and therefore whether projects are socially valuable or not. If we assume that V_h is not known at the constitutional stage, we have to use a flexible majority rule in order to achieve a first-best allocation. To make the working of this rule more transparent, we will use a slightly different representation of the rule for socially efficient public project provision:

$$g = 1 \text{ if and only if } V_h > V_h^*, \text{ where}$$
$$V_h^* := \min\{V_h \geq 0 \,|\, p\,V_h + (1-p)V_l \geq (1+\lambda)k\}$$

and taxes are raised solely to finance the public project.

Hence, for given p, V_l and project costs $(1+\lambda)k$, the utility level V_h^* is the smallest benefit level at which it is socially beneficial to provide the public project. We obtain:

Proposition 10.2
Suppose that V_h is not known at the constitutional stage. Then the constitution

$$CO_3 := \{[CA(b)], [NS], [TMf(p\,(n_T \leq q^*), 1)]\}$$

$$\textit{with} \quad q^* = \frac{k(1+\lambda)}{V_h^*}$$
and b sufficiently high

is first-best.

Proposition 10.2 indicates that a first best allocation can be achieved by the combination of costly agenda setting, a ban on subsidies, and flexible majority rules. Essentially, an agenda setter is able to form a majority if and only if $V_h \geq V_h^*$, since he can tax a fraction of q^* individuals by $t = V_h^*$ which is sufficient to finance the public project. Since tax rates are not higher than V_h^*, taxed project-winners still support the proposal. The high costs of agenda setting deter project-losers from applying for agenda setting and proposing $g = 0$, since project-losers do not know whether V_h is larger or smaller than V_h^*. A project-winner will apply for agenda setting if and only if he observes that V_h is larger than V_h^* and $g = 1$ can be therefore implemented. The fact that individuals cannot observe the utilities of other agents makes it possible to set agenda costs so high that project-losers will not want to face the risk of defeat.

10.4.3 Uncertainty Regarding p

In this section we assume that individuals do not know whether they benefit from the public project at the constitutional stage, and how large the share of project-winners is. Now the problem becomes more subtle since neither a project-winner nor a project loser can observe the proportion of project-winners and thus whether a proposal is likely to be accepted or not. Nevertheless, a modified constitution will ensure that a first-best allocation can be achieved. Again we represent the first-best public project provision rule in a convenient way.

$$g = 1 \quad \text{if and only if} \quad p \geq p^*, \quad \text{where}$$

$$p^* := \min\{p \geq 0 \,|\, p\,V_h + (1-p)\,V_l \geq (1+\lambda)\,k\},$$

$$p^* = \frac{(1+\lambda)k - V_l}{V_h - V_l}$$

$$s_j = 0 \quad \text{for all } j$$

We use $Pr\{p \geq p^*\}$ and $Pr\{p < p^*\}$ to denote the probabilities that the share of project-winners is larger and smaller than p^*, respectively. The probabilities must be known at the constitutional stage. We obtain

Proposition 10.3

Suppose that p is not known at the constitutional stage and that

$$-V_l \leq \frac{Pr\{p \geq p^*\}(1+\lambda)k}{Pr\{p < p^*\}}$$

Then the constitution

$$CO_4 := \Big\{[CA(b)]\,, [NS]\,, \big[TMf\big(p^*(n_T \leq p^*), 1\big)\big]\Big\}$$

where b must fulfill

$$-V_l \leq b \leq \frac{Pr\{p \geq p^*\}(1+\lambda)k}{Pr\{p < p^*\}}$$

is first-best.

When there is only uncertainty about p, there is no possibility of deterring project-losers from setting the agenda by making agenda costs prohibitively high, as this will act as a deterrent for everyone. Moreover, it follows from proposition 10.3 that the constitutional problem is already sufficiently delicate if p is not known at the constitutional stage, because the successful implementation of CO_4 depends on parameters.

10.4.4 Higher Dimensional Uncertainty

In this section we suggest that a higher dimensional uncertainty about the project parameters – e.g. who benefits, how large the benefits are and how large the share of beneficiaries is – may make it possible to design rules under a veil of ignorance to achieve first-best allocations. Consider for example the problem when the size of the benefits from public projects and the proportion of project-winners are not known at the constitutional stage. As shown in Gersbach (2002) the joint uncertainty about V_h and p can make it easier to achieve first-best allocations. The additional uncertainty about V_h makes it possible to set flexible agenda costs at a level such that project-losers do not apply for agenda setting in equilibrium because they do not know V_h, whereas project-winners do. Such a deterrence of project-losers from agenda setting is desirable since project-losers have an incentive to prevent the adoption of socially desirable projects by making unattractive proposals.

10.5 Discussion and Alternative Democratic Mechanisms

10.5.1 Dictatorial Agenda Setting

The preceding section indicates that democratic constitutions become more complex the more uncertainty dimensions are present. The main reason for the rapidly increasing sophistication of rules is that all four potential inefficiencies identified in section 10.3.2 need to be overcome by democratic mechanisms. If only the fourth and the first two inefficiencies needed to be dealt with, much simpler first-best mechanisms would exist. To illustrate the claim we consider a hypothetical situation. Suppose that the agenda is set by a benevolent dictator. Then the third source of inefficiency would be automatically avoided and we could consider the following game.

Stage 1: In the constitutional period, society decides unanimously about the constitutional principles governing legislative decision-making.

Stage 2: At the start of the legislative period, the benevolent agenda setter proposes a project/financing package $(g, t_j, s_j)_{j \in [0,1]}$. Denote this choice by A_a.

Stage 3: Given A_a, citizens decide whether to accept the proposal $(\delta_j(A_a) = 1)$ or not $(\delta_j(A_a) = 0)$.

As an example for simpler mechanisms, we explore the design of constitutions when there is uncertainty about winners and losers and uncertainty regarding the share of project-winners, i.e. uncertainty regarding p. Then, we obtain:

Proposition 10.4

Suppose that p is not known at the constitutional stage and agenda setting is dictatorial and benevolent. Then the constitution

$$CO_5 = \{[NS], [M(p^*)]\}$$

where

$$p^* := \min \{p \geq 0 \,|\, p V_h + (1-p) V_l \geq (1+\lambda)k\}$$

is first-best.

Proposition 10.4 follows directly from the observation that a benevolent agenda setter proposes $g = 1$ if and only if $p \geq p^*$

and in this case can set the tax rates $t = (1 + \lambda)k$ for all individuals.

Several remarks need to be made at this point. First, it is important that the benevolent agenda setter maximizes aggregate utility and therefore proposes projects if welfare in a utilitarian sense can be improved although project losers are worse off compared to the status quo. Second, under benevolent and dictatorial agenda setting the ban on subsidies, NS, in constitution CO_5 could even be dropped.

Note that, if agenda setting is determined randomly and thus all agents have the same chance to set the agenda as in the previous sections, the constitution CO_5 is not first-best. All individuals would apply for agenda setting. If a project-loser could determine the agenda, he would propose $g = 0$ since, because of NS, he loses when the project is adopted. This problem could only be avoided by dropping NS, but then inefficiencies arise from excessive taxation to generate subsidies, thus increasing tax distortions. Therefore, the simple mechanism in this section does not yield first-best allocations under democratic agenda setting.

Third, when there is additional uncertainty about V_h the dictatorial and benevolent agenda setter might not be able to use simpler constitutions to achieve first-best allocations. This is left for future research.

10.5.2 Equal Treatment Rules

An important feature of the constitutions considered so far is that individuals can be – and are – treated differently with respect to taxation. An agenda setter can make non-anonymous proposals and can impose different taxes on individuals. In this section we consider whether this feature is vital to our arguments. For this purpose we consider two constitutional treatment rules. As in chapter 9, we denote by ETT the requirement that a proposal is only constitutional if all individuals are treated equally with respect to taxes, i.e. t_j is the same for all individuals. Moreover, we denote by $ETTaxed$ the treatment rule which means that all individuals who are taxed (i.e. for whom $t_j > 0$) must be treated equally with respect to taxation. As proposition 10.3 illustrates, imposing $ETTaxed$ in addition to the constitutions under consideration would not destroy the first-best allocation because equilibrium proposals satisfy $ETTaxed$ and further constraints on out-of-equilibrium strategies do not destroy the equilibrium.

The situation is different, however, if ETT is imposed. Then, proposals cannot vary in terms of the fraction of taxed individual n_T or in the pattern of taxation or subsidization across agents. Hence, the potential of flexible majority rules cannot be exploited and inefficiencies occur.

10.5.3 Only Project-Winners

Throughout this chapter we have assumed $V_l < 0$ and that project-losers indeed are harmed by the project. But it is also important to see how the democratic mechanisms need to be adjusted in the case $V_l \geq 0$. It is obvious that all constitutions can be applied for $V_l \geq 0$ as well. The only exception is proposition 10.1, where agenda setting costs can be skipped or be set as $CA(\max\{[0, -V_l]\})$ for the general case when V_l can be positive or negative.

There exists, however, an important difference between $V_l > 0$ and $V_l < 0$. In the case $V_l > 0$, it may not be necessary to deter agents from agenda setting since they can always benefit potentially from $g = 1$ by proposing zero taxes for themselves. Therefore, simpler mechanisms may again be first-best in the case $V_l > 0$. As an example, suppose that $V_l > 0$ and p is not known at the constitutional stage. Then, since agents with V_h or V_l will propose $g = 1$ if they can determine the agenda (including zero taxes for themselves), the simple constitution $CO_5 = \{[NS], [M(p^*)]\}$ will implement the first-best allocation. However, if there is uncertainty regarding V_h and p, such simple constitutions may not be first-best since deterrence from agenda setting becomes again important.

10.6 Conclusions

Our analysis suggests that democracies, viewed as the liberal-democracy constraint on the set of social mechanisms, can deliver socially desirable results if agenda-cost rules are combined with flexible and double majority rules.

There are a number of extensions that should be taken up by future research. First, how can the ideas in this chapter be applied to situations with an arbitrary number of different utility levels from the project? By setting the minimal tax at a sufficiently high level, it will still be possible to deter all individuals who do not receive the highest project benefits from applying for agenda setting. But whether precise socially efficient implementation can be achieved is unclear, since taxation of intermediate beneficiaries cannot be tailored to their actual benefit level, this being unobservable for agenda setters.

Second, how robust is the principle that higher dimensional uncertainty can make it easier to achieve socially optimal allocations? Our current conjecture is that it is impossible to design a constitution under the liberal-democracy constraint which implements a first-best allocation if there is uncertainty about all project parameters. If this conjecture is true, our results could suggest a role for constitutional courts in the provision of public projects. That role would be an assessment of negative utilities from a public project in order to allow the efficient working of democratic constitutions.

Third, will the possibility of amendments or second proposals at the legislative stage help to generate better outcomes? Again in this chapter, such counterproposals are not necessary, indeed they are unwelcome, since individuals who gain less from a proposal than others have the opportunity to wait for better proposals which, in turn, could lead to rejections of socially desirable proposals. From a broader perspective, however, amendments may serve a variety of useful purposes such as enhanced information aggregation and easiness of achieving distributional objectives. Broadening the scope of democratic mechanisms in these directions are fruitful research questions.

Fourth, flexible and double majority rules require open ballots and are therefore best suited for smaller communities. As discussed in the last chapter, the internet could alleviate the practical implementation problems of democratic constitutions considered in this book.

11. Fair Division[1]

11.1 Introduction

While we have focused solely on allocative issues in the last chapter we now address in addition distributional objectives. We suggest that flexible majority rules, where the necessary majority for the adoption of a proposal depends on the distributional implication of the proposal, may overcome the disadvantages of collective decision rules in achieving distributional objectives when they are coupled with agenda rights for the opposition or exclusion of repeated agenda setting.

We consider the distribution of resources by a collective choice process in a dynamic model with endogenous agenda setting in the spirit of the contributions by Baron and Ferejohn (1989), Harrington (1990), Harrington (1986), Banks and Gasmi (1987), Ferejohn, Fiorina, and McKelvey (1987) and Epple and Riordan (1987)). A community of N individuals decides on how to distribute resources. The group meets for a finite or an infinite number of periods. Individuals are impatient, implying that waiting is costly. In each period, an agent is chosen according to some recognition rule. A proposal is accepted or rejected by a flexible majority rule. If the proposal is accepted, resources are allocated and the process is terminated; otherwise it continues.

[1] A version of this chapter has appeared in Gersbach (2004a).

Under a flexible majority rule, the required majority is derived from the proposal: the larger the difference between the shares of the cake across individuals, the larger the majority needed to adopt a proposal is. As an example, consider the polar case of a threshold flexible majority rule in the following sense: The simple majority rule applies as long as the maximal difference in resources across individuals is below a certain threshold; otherwise the unanimity rule applies.

This investigation is motivated by a large literature on the advantages and disadvantages of the unanimity rule.[2] Wicksell (1896) was the first to link the potential for all to benefit from collective action to the unanimity rule. The unanimity rule is the only voting rule that always leads to Pareto-efficient public project quantities and tax schemes if no delay of decisions occurs, as recognized by Wicksell (1896)[3] and in the classic contribution of Buchanan and Tullock (1965) (see Mueller (1989) for a comprehensive survey). Two main criticisms have been made against the unanimity rule.[4]

First, searching for a Pareto-efficient allocation might take considerable time, particularly in large communities with diverse interests. The time required to define an issue and transaction costs to reach an agreement may become so high as to wipe out the benefits from full cooperation under the unanimity rule.

Second, the unanimity rule invites strategic behavior: an individual strategically vetoes a proposal in order to seek a greater share of the gains from collective action (see Black (1958), Buchanan and Tullock (1965), Barry (1965), Samuelson (1969)). Because of

[2] See Buchanan (1991) and Mueller (1996) for general surveys on constitutional political economy.

[3] Also, the famous Lindahl equilibrium (Lindahl (1958)) could be reached under the unanimity rule.

[4] Buchanan and Tullock (1965) identify such disadvantages as external costs of decision-making.

these objections, even scientists most favorably disposed towards the unanimity rule have argued to abandon this principle.

However, the simple or super majority rules are plagued with drawbacks as well. In particular, majority rules can lead to the exploitation of minorities. The distribution of the benefits reflects the majoritarian distribution of power in that only a minimal majority of individuals receives a positive allocation of benefits.[5] Moreover, from an *ex ante* or constitutional point of view, the risk of being exploited by majorities may lead to Pareto-inefficient allocations if voters are risk averse.

In this chapter, we suggest that flexible majority rules might alleviate the drawbacks of the unanimity rule and the majority rule in distributing resources in a society. Suppose the polity uses a flexible majority rule where the size of the majority increases continuously or even jumps with the maximal difference between the benefits individuals receive. For large discount factors, such flexible majority rules lead to an efficient and even distribution of resources although the simple majority rule governs the collective choice process in equilibrium. A proposal with a more unequal distribution of benefits would require a larger majority or even the unanimity rule, making it unattractive for an agenda setter. For low discount rates, or when individuals are uncertain about each other's discount rates, efficient and envy-free divisions of resources can still be achieved if flexible majority rules are combined with agenda setting rules, such as the right of a minority to set future agendas or the exclusion of repeated agenda setting. While this chapter provides a sequence of examples, a comprehensive theory

[5] However, institutional arrangements and amendment rules which govern majoritarian bodies such as legislatures can lead to more universal distributions of resources and may act as a substitute to the flexible majority rules suggested in this chapter (see Shepsle (1979), Weingast (1979) and Baron and Ferejohn (1989)).

about flexible majority rules and appropriate agenda rules must still be developed. In the last section we will discuss how further research could close this gap.

The work in this chapter is related to further strands of literature. First, efficiency and fairness of distribution of resources has been studied under alternative collective choice processes. Mueller (1978) and Moulin (1981) examined the veto rule. In the case of no agreement, resources are thrown away. Equilibria in such games show a strong tendency towards equal shares for each individual. We are concerned with the possibility of using majority rules and only one proposal at each voting stage to create efficient and evenly distributed benefits of collective choices.

Second, flexible majority rules, where the size of the majority depends on the share of taxed people, were introduced in the last chapters to achieve socially optimal allocations of public projects from a constitutional perspective. In this chapter, we introduce flexible majority rules that depend directly on the different levels of benefits individual agents receive in a collective choice process.

We can reach efficiency and envy-freeness with flexible majority rules and agenda setting rules. However, it is important that an outside agency such as a court or a special committee in a legislature can observe and verify the benefits received by individuals which is not possible in all circumstances in actual decisions. In particular, applying flexible majority rules for policies in legislatures is not possible in all cases, since benefits might not be verifiable. Moreover, the examination of institutional structures of legislatures (Shepsle (1979), Weingast (1979), Ferejohn, Fiorina, and McKelvey (1987), Gilligan and Krehbiel (1987), Baron and Ferejohn (1989)) suggest that agenda amendment rules can have a great impact on legislative outcomes even within the standard majority-rule framework. How flexible majority rules could and should be embedded in an institutional framework for legislatures remains an open issue.

Finally, our discussion is related to the fairness approaches how resources should be divided. The question of fair-division procedures that allow for sharing of divisible resources has received a lot of attention in recent years as developed and summarized in important contributions by Moulin (1995), Brams and Taylor (1996), Robertson and Webb (1998). Since, in this chapter, individuals are identical with respect to their preferences, we use efficiency and envy-freeness as criteria for assessing allocations of collective choice processes. Our suggestion to use flexible majority rules in collective choice processes might complement this work on fairness.

The chapter is organized as follows. In the next section we introduce the model. Section 11.3 deals with the division of resources within a finite number of periods. In section 11.4, we discuss how the results change under an infinite time horizon. Section 11.5 presents our conclusion.

11.2 The Model

We consider the problem of a group of N individuals (N odd and $N > 1$) distributing a cake of one unit among themselves. All individuals are assumed to be risk-neutral and have utility functions

$$U_i = \sum_{t=1}^{\infty} \delta^t \, x_i^t$$

where x_i^t is the share of the cake individual i receives in period t. Since the cake can only be distributed once, x_i^t can only be positive for one period at most.[6] δ $(0 < \delta < 1)$ is the discount factor which, in the first part of the chapter, will be assumed to be identical across individuals. The distribution of the cake is governed by a collective choice process containing a voting rule, and by a recognition rule that determines which individual may make a proposal. Later, we supplement the collective choice process by agenda rules. We assume that a particular distribution of the cake does not affect the size of the cake.[7] The socially optimal or Pareto-efficient solutions require that the whole cake is distributed in $t = 1$.

As in many other instances, Pareto-efficiency is not sufficient to describe all characteristics of socially desired allocations. In particular, we will apply the no-envy test, which is the dominant argument of justice in microeconomic theory.[8] Of course, the no-envy test in our simple problem requires each individual to receive the same share $\frac{1}{N}$ of the cake since utility functions of all individuals are identical.

Society uses flexible majority rules to distribute the cake. A flexible majority rule $F : [0;1] \to [0;1]$ requires the share of votes necessary to adopt a proposal to be at least $F(\Delta x)$, where:

$$\Delta x := \max_{i,j} |x_i - x_j|$$

This is the most simple formulation of flexible majority rules, depending only on the maximal difference between the benefits two individuals receive. Any measure of the extent how benefits

6 Theoretically, it would be possible to distribute the cake partially over many periods which is inefficient and does not occur in equilibria. Therefore this possibility is neglected in our analysis.

7 This is a restrictive assumption for allocation problems in practice.

8 The no-envy test was stated by Foley (1967) and has been further developed by Kolm (1972) and Varian (1974). Moulin (1995) provides a comprehensive discussion of the pros and cons of the no-envy test.

are distributed could be used to define flexible majority rules. We give the following three examples for majority rules:

- *constant majority rule with a necessary majority* $\alpha(\alpha \in [0,1])$:

$$F_{\alpha}^{C}(\Delta x) = \alpha$$

- *threshold flexible majority rule with parameters* α, $(\alpha \in [0,1])$ *and* $\beta(\beta \geq 0)$:

$$F_{\alpha,\beta}^{T}(\Delta x) = \begin{cases} 1 & \text{if} \quad \Delta x > \beta \\ \alpha & \text{otherwise} \end{cases}$$

- *linear flexible majority rule with the slope* α:

$$F_{\alpha}^{L}(\Delta x) = \frac{1}{2} + \alpha\Delta x \qquad \text{with} \quad \alpha \in [0;1/2]$$

Note that a threshold flexible majority rule jumps from an α–majority rule to an unanimity rule as soon as individuals receive shares of the cake differing by more than β from the shares of other individuals. We consider the following sequence of events within a particular period:

Stage 1: An individual is randomly chosen to set the agenda. The agenda setter in period t, a^t, proposes an allocation of the cake $x_a^t = (x_1^t, \cdots, x_N^t)$ with $\sum_{i=1}^{N} x_i^t \leq 1$, so that the set $\mathcal{X}$ of feasible proposals is an N–dimensional simplex.

Stage 2: The corresponding majority decision rule for x_a^t is determined and individuals cast their votes. If the proposal receives a majority, the process is terminated. Otherwise, the collective choice process continues in the next period.

In the following we will explore the collective choice process with finite and infinite periods. Following Baron and Ferejohn (1989) we will restrict attention to subgame-perfect equilibria, in which weakly dominated strategies are eliminated.[9] Moreover, we assume the following tie-breaking rule: If an agent is indifferent between supporting and rejecting a proposal, the agent will vote yes. The tie-breaking rule is not crucial for the results.

11.3 A Finite Number of Periods

11.3.1 Random Recognition

To illustrate the basic structure of the model and the way flexible majority rules work, consider a simple case of a two-period collective choice process with equal probabilities of recognition for each individual, i.e. each individual will have the same likelihood of setting the agenda. We assume that if by the end of the allocation process no proposal has been accepted, each individual receives zero benefits.[10] In a finite number of periods we can work backwards to derive the subgame-perfect equilibria. We obtain:

Proposition 11.1

Suppose that society uses a threshold flexible majority rule with a threshold of $\beta = 1 - \delta$ to distribute resources. Then, there is a unique subgame-perfect equilibrium of the two-period collective choice process:

(i) The individual recognized in the first period, i.e. the agenda setter a, proposes

[9] This assumption is standard because of the coarseness of voting rules. The refinement significantly reduces the multiplicity of equilibria and is, therefore, a critical assumption.

[10] This is not plausible in all cases since there might exist a default distribution of benefits. As long as, however, the community does not realize some social gains at the end of the collective choice process, we can transform the problem into our framework by an appropriate normalization.

$$x_a = 1 - \frac{N-1}{N}\delta,\ x_i = \frac{\delta}{N},\ i \neq a$$

(ii) Society uses the simple majority rule to decide on the proposal in the first period. The first proposal is thus accepted and the collective choice process is adjourned in the first period.

Proof

Because the group decision is terminated after two periods, each individual of the group votes for any second-period proposal. The individual recognized at the beginning of period 2 can thus successfully propose to take the whole cake since each individual will vote for it because her expected utility is zero anyway. According to our tie-breaking rule, the proposal will be unanimously supported. Although the unanimity rule applies, the agenda setter can extract all benefits in the second period. Her benefits are therefore given by δ. Since each individual has a probability $\frac{1}{N}$ of being recognized in the second period, expected utility amounts to $\frac{\delta}{N}$ if the proposal is rejected in the first period. As a consequence, each individual votes for any first-period proposal in which she receives at least $\frac{\delta}{N}$. Therefore, the proposal will be adopted.

It remains to be shown that the proposal is indeed optimal for the agenda setter. Note that in equilibrium

$$\Delta x := \max_{i,j} |x_i - x_j| = x_a - x_i = 1 - \delta.$$

Therefore, the simple majority rule applies. If the recognized individual tried to increase her utility by increasing x_a, Δx would necessarily be above the given threshold. Thus, the unanimity rule would apply and the proposal would be rejected since at least one individual would receive resources below $\frac{\delta}{N}$. Of course, the agenda setter does not want the proposal to be rejected since, according to her proposal, she receives a utility of $1 - \frac{N-1}{N}\delta > \frac{\delta}{N}$ instead of an expected utility $\frac{\delta}{N}$ when the proposal is not accepted.

□

It is instructive to compare our results with those of Baron and Ferejohn (1989), who have examined the same model for the simple majority rule. Under the simple majority rule, an agenda setter in the first period distributes $\frac{\delta}{N}$ to $\frac{(N-1)}{2}$ other individuals and keeps $1 - \frac{\delta(N-1)}{2N}$ for himself.[11] Although the simple majority rule governs the collective choice process in our context, every individual receives at least $\frac{\delta}{N}$.[12] More unequal distributions of resources would imply that the unanimity rule applies and such proposals would be rejected. Flexible majority rules yield a more equal distribution of benefits although the simple majority rule governs the voting process in equilibrium.

11.3.2 Agenda Rules and Equal Distribution

While flexible majority rules yield an efficient, relatively even, distribution of benefits if the discount factor is sufficiently large, the agenda setter in the first period can extract most of the surplus if discount factors are low. In this case, the flexible majority rule supplemented by agenda setting rules still guarantees equal or almost equal distributions of benefits. We explore the following agenda setting rule:

OAS: Opposition Agenda Setting

In the first period, each individual has the same likelihood of de-

[11] Under the unanimity rule the same distribution of resources as under the threshold flexible majority rule is achieved.

[12] See Herrero (1985) for an analysis of the unanimity rule for an infinite number of periods.

termining the agenda. In the second period, only individuals who have voted against the proposal can apply for agenda setting.[13]

Each individual who can apply for agenda setting has the same chance of being recognized.

Such agenda setting features create higher incentives to reject proposals in the first period which, in turn, induces agenda setters to propose more uniform distributions. By tailoring the flexible majority rule to the agenda setting rule, we obtain:

Proposition 11.2
Suppose $\delta \geq \frac{1}{N}$ and OAS. There is then a flexible threshold majority rule $F^{T}_{\alpha,0}(\Delta x)$ that yields a subgame-perfect equilibrium in which the agenda setter in the first period proposes:

$$x = \left(\frac{1}{N}, \ldots, \frac{1}{N}\right)$$

The agenda setter's proposal is accepted by an α–majority rule. α is given by:

$$\alpha = \frac{N - n^*}{N} \quad \textit{with } n^* = [\delta\, N]^{14}$$

The proof of proposition 11.2 is given in the appendix. The important point of proposition 11.2 is that flexible majority rules and opposition agenda setting yield an efficient and an envy-free allocation for low discount factors. Although only an α-majority rule is applied in equilibrium, any other proposal by the agenda setter requires the unanimity rule and, because of strategic rejection, will not be adopted by the community. Strategic rejection describes the fact that under OAS individuals have a strong incentive to reject a proposal in order to determine the agenda in

13 Obviously, the anonymity of voters is not possible for this agenda rule to be applied and voting needs to take place openly and sequentially.

14 This means the maximal natural number smaller or equal than $\delta\, N$.

the future if all other individuals support the proposal under consideration.

11.3.3 Uncertainty About Discount Factors

Flexible majority rules can also operate differently than simple majority rules when there is uncertainty about other individual's discount factors. Suppose that the discount factor of agents is either $\delta_H = 1$ or $\delta_L < 1$. The probability of an individual having a discount factor δ^H (δ^L) is common knowledge and denoted by p_H (p_L). Each individual can only observe her own discount factor. Suppose that the society uses a threshold flexible majority rule with parameters $\alpha = \frac{1}{2}$ and $\beta = 0$.

Uncertainty about discount factors requires new considerations, since agenda setters can try to gamble. We will illustrate this point by the following example.

Assume $N = 3$. The expected utility for the individual under consideration is $\frac{\delta_H}{N} = \frac{1}{N}$ or $\frac{\delta_L}{N}$, respectively, if her first-period proposal is rejected. Now assume that the individual proposes $x = (\frac{N-2\delta_L}{N}, \frac{\delta_L}{N}, \frac{\delta_L}{N})$, where the first entry of the vector defines the benefits the agenda setter would like to donate to herself. This proposal would not be rejected by individuals with low discount factors. The recognized individual receives a share that is larger than $1/N$. With probability $(p_L)^2$, both remaining individuals have low discount factors and will accept the proposal. Expected benefits from the proposal for an agenda setter with discount rate $\delta_a \in \left\{\delta_H, \delta_L\right\}$ amount to:

$$(p_L)^2\left(1 - \frac{(2\delta_L)}{N}\right) + \left(1 - (p_L)^2\right)\frac{\delta_a}{N}$$

Whether the proposal $x = \left(\frac{N-2\delta_L}{N}, \frac{\delta_L}{N}, \frac{\delta_L}{N}\right)$ is profitable for an agenda setter compared, for instance, to $x = \left(\frac{1}{N}, \frac{1}{N}, \frac{1}{N}\right)$ depends on the discount rate. Suppose that the agenda setter has $\delta_a = \delta_L$. Then, the comparison yields that the agenda setter proposes $\left(\frac{1}{N}, \frac{1}{N}, \frac{1}{N}\right)$ if and only if

$$p_L \leq \frac{1}{\sqrt{3}}$$

The agenda setter could also propose $x = \left(1 - \frac{1}{N} - \frac{\delta_L}{N}, \frac{1}{N}, \frac{\delta_L}{N}\right)$ with a winning probability p_L. This proposal yields a higher expected utility than the efficient and envy-free proposal $\left(\frac{1}{N}, \frac{1}{N}, \frac{1}{N}\right)$ if $p_L > \frac{1}{2}$. Therefore, as long as $p_L \leq \frac{1}{2}$, an agenda setter with $\delta_a = \delta_L$ will not gamble by the proposal $x = \left(1 - \frac{1}{N} - \frac{\delta_L}{N}, \frac{1}{N}, \frac{\delta_L}{N}\right)$. To sum up, as long as $p_L > \frac{1}{2}$, the agenda setter will gamble which creates the risk that the distribution of resources will be delayed. Consider an individual with discount rate $\delta_H = 1$ who is recognized to set the agenda in the first period. Since

$$(p_L)^2\left(1 - \frac{2\,\delta_L}{N}\right) + (1 - (p_L)^2)\frac{1}{N} > \frac{1}{N}$$

such an agenda setter will always propose $x = \left(\frac{N-2\delta_L}{N}, \frac{\delta_L}{N}, \frac{\delta_L}{N}\right)$ instead of $x = \left(\frac{1}{N}, \frac{1}{N}, \frac{1}{N}\right)$. Her proposal will be accepted with probability $(p_L)^2$. However, this proposal does not only violate envy-freeness, but it is also inefficient, since there is a positive probability that resources are distributed in the second period.

In order to achieve efficient and envy-free distributions of benefits when discount rates are uncertain, we can complement the flexible majority rule and the random recognition rule by a simple agenda right rule.

ERAS: Exclusion of Repeated Agenda Setting
The individual that was allowed to set the agenda in the first period is excluded from agenda setting in the second period.

This assumption makes gambling much less attractive. The individual under recognition knows that her utility is zero if her proposal is rejected. Thus it is not beneficial to deviate from proposal $x = (\frac{1}{N}, \frac{1}{N}, \frac{1}{N})$. One can show:

Proposition 11.3
Suppose that the discount factor of an individual is either $\delta_H = 1$ or $\delta_L \leq \frac{N-1}{N}$. Suppose that the community uses a threshold flexible majority rule $F^T_{\frac{1}{2},0}$ and ERAS. Then, a unique equilibrium exists, where the recognized individual, acting independently from her discount factor, proposes the distribution:

$$x = \left(\frac{1}{N}, \ldots, \frac{1}{N}\right)$$

if $0 < p_L \leq p_L^*$ for some $p_L^* > 0$. The simple majority rule applies, and the proposal is accepted if there are at least $\frac{N-1}{2}$ individuals who have δ_L.

Proposition 11.3 indicates that flexible majority rules can lead to efficient and uniform distribution of resources if repeated agenda setting by individuals is excluded and if the chance that individuals have a low discount factor is not too high. The exclusion of repeated agenda setting is a plausible agenda rule. With such a simple agenda setting rule, agenda setters cannot risk to propose uneven proposals because the unanimity rule would be applied and the proposal might be rejected. In this respect, uncertainty about discount rates is favorable for the community to achieve efficient and envy-free allocations.

11.4 Division of Resources with Infinite Periods

When the number of periods is infinite, it is well known that any distribution of benefits may be supported as a subgame-perfect equilibrium if agents are not too impatient. Following the literature (see, e.g., Baron and Ferejohn (1989)), we focus on stationary equilibria or Markov equilibria. We are interested in whether the qualitative results in the last section carry over to collective choice processes with infinite periods.

Proposition 11.4
Suppose that society uses threshold flexible majority rules $F^T_{\frac{1}{2},1-\delta}(\Delta x)$ and a random recognition rule. Then, a unique stationary equilibrium exists in which any agenda setter proposes

$$x_a = 1 - (N-1)\frac{\delta}{N}$$

$$x_i = \frac{\delta}{N}, \quad i \neq a$$

Each individual votes for any proposal in which at least $\frac{\delta}{N}$ is received. The simple majority rule applies and the proposal is accepted in the first period.

The proof of proposition 11.4 is given in the appendix. Proposition 11.4 indicates that our results carry over to infinite horizons, at least in the simple cases we have considered. Introducing agenda setting rules without the random recognition rule, however, makes the derivation of stationary equilibria more complicated. Whether the simple intuitions for the combination of flexible majority rules and agenda setting rules for finite periods carry over to infinite periods remains open and will be explored in future research.

11.5 Discussion and Conclusions

In this chapter, we have used the novel social choice rules, namely flexible majority rules, to distribute resources in larger communities. These rules combine the advantages of majority rules of being simple and avoiding strategic delay with the advantages of unanimity rules of yielding even distributions. The functioning of the flexible majority rules is intuitively understandable. In order to avoid very uneven distributions, the majority required for adopting a proposal increases with the amount of inequality a proposal creates. This makes it much harder for proposals to win elections when they imply a very heterogeneous distribution of resources. As a consequence, the combination of flexible majority rules and agenda setting rules can yield efficient and envy-free allocations.

Further research is necessary to investigate how and if flexible majority rules could be applied in actual political processes when resources are distributed. Flexible majority rules must be stated rather generally to be able to be applied in a large variety of contexts. Moreover, flexible majority rules require the computation of the utility spread Δx, which must be evaluated by an independent institution. Since this may seem rather difficult in some cases, it is desirable to search for other variables which can be measured more easily and can approximate the utility spread. Finally, it must be examined how flexible majority rules can be applied when individuals differ strongly in their preferences and more than one commodity has to be allocated among a set of individuals.

11.6 Appendix

Proof of proposition 11.2

Similar to the proof of proposition 11.1, an individual that is recognized in the second period proposes to keep the whole cake. Society will accept this proposal since all other individuals will receive zero utility anyhow. Thus, utility for an agenda setting individual in the second period amounts to δ.

We use n to denote the number of individuals refusing the first-period proposal. Hence, first-period expected utility for an individual refusing the first period proposal is $\frac{\delta}{n}$ if the first-period proposal will be rejected.

Now assume that the following flexible majority rule is used:

$$F^T_{\alpha,0}(\Delta x) = \begin{cases} 1 & \text{if} \quad \Delta x > 0 \\ \alpha & \text{if} \quad \Delta x = 0 \end{cases}$$

α is left to be determined. We use n^* to denote the number of individuals voting against the proposal in equilibrium. If no additional individual wants to vote "no" and no individual voting "yes" wants to change her position, the following inequality must hold:

$$\frac{\delta}{n^* + 1} \leq \frac{1}{N} \leq \frac{\delta}{n^*}.$$

If δN is not a natural number, n^* is uniquely determined. If δN is a natural number, n^* is either δN or $\delta N - 1$. Hence, α, which is the fraction of individuals voting "yes" necessary to adopt the proposal, is given by:

$$\alpha = \frac{N - n^*}{N}$$

By construction, no individual benefits from changing her voting behavior. It remains to be shown that no proposal exists that would yield higher benefits for the recognized individual.

Clearly, the above proposal is more attractive than any proposal that would be rejected. If the recognized individual chose a different distribution of benefits with a larger share of the cake for herself, the unanimity rule would apply. But such a proposal would invite strategic rejection. If all other individuals accept the proposal, incentives to vote "no" are extremely strong for one individual, since the opposing individual could receive all of the benefits in the next period. The condition that such strategic rejection does not occur is

$$\delta \geq \frac{1}{N}$$

which is true for most plausible values of N[15] and δ and is assumed in the proposition.

□

Proof of proposition 11.4[16]

It is obvious that the configuration of proposals and voting strategies is an equilibrium in any subgame. In order to establish necessity, suppose that w denotes the stationary expected continuation for an individual value when the proposal in the first period is rejected. Since all individuals are identical at the beginning of period 2, expected continuation values are equal for all individuals. Consider the proposal made by an individual in the first period. Any individual receiving $x_i \geq \delta w$ will vote for such a proposal.

[15] It is important to note that equilibria exist where n individuals vote "no" for every n with $0 \leq n \leq n^*$. These equilibria yield the same distribution of resources since the proposal is always accepted.

[16] The proof uses considerations similar to those used in Baron and Ferejohn (1989) for the simple majority rule.

Because of the flexible-majority rule requirement, suppose that the agenda setter offers $x_i = \delta w$ for all individuals in period 1. Then, expected utility for all individuals amounts to

$$w = \frac{1}{N}[1 - (N-1)\delta w] + \frac{N-1}{N}\delta w$$

which implies $w = \frac{1}{N}, x_a = 1 - \frac{N-1}{N}\delta$ and $x_i = \frac{\delta}{N}$ for $i \neq a$. We have $\max|x_a - x_i| = 1 - \delta$ and the simple majority prevails.

Note that it is impossible for the agenda setter to increase her share of the cake. An increase in x_a necessarily implies that $x_i < \frac{\delta}{N}$ for at least one individual. Therefore, since $\max|x_a - x_i|$ would be greater than $1 - \delta$ the unanimity rule applies. But since $x_i < \delta w$ for at least one individual, the proposal will be rejected and the agenda setter is worse off than with the equilibrium proposal.

□

Epilogue to Part II

The second part of the book has developed the idea that democratic mechanisms - understood as an appropriate combination of agenda, decision, and agenda setter rules - can provide citizens with the laws and public projects they want. Ultimately, this is a belief, but it proves well-founded when we transcend the details of many models of democracy and combine the history of accumulated wisdom with economic theory. However, it would be a grave mistake not to continue to search for innovative ways of improving liberal democracies. Although the democratic system is the best form of government and the best mechanism for controlling the power monopoly of the state, it still needs to evolve as society develops. The ideas in the second part may help to explore some of the paths that democratic procedures can take.

References to Part II

AGHION, P., and P. BOLTON (1998): *Incomplete Social Contract.* (mimeo).

ALIPRANTIS, C., and K. BORDER (2000): *Infinite Dimensional Analysis: A Hitchhikers's Guide.* Springer, Heidelberg.

ARROW, K. (1951): *Social Choice and Individual Values.* Yale University Press, New Haven.

——— (1979): "The Property Rights Doctrine and Demand Revelation Under Incomplete Information," in *Economics and Human Welfare.* Academic Press, New York.

AUSTEN-SMITH, D., and J. BANKS (1996): "Information Aggregation, Rationality and the Condorcet Jury Theorem," *American Political Science Review*, 90, 34–45.

BANKS, J., and F. GASMI (1987): "Endogenous Agenda Formation in Three-Person Committees," *Social Choice and Welfare*, 4, 133–152.

BARBERA, S., and O. JACKSON (2000): "Choosing How to Choose: Self-Stable Majority Rules," California Institute of Technology, Pasadena, Mimeo.

BARON, D., and J. FEREJOHN (1989): "Bargaining in Legislatures," *American Political Science Review*, 83(4), 1181–1206.

BARRY, B. (1965): *Political Argument.* Routledge and Kegan Paul, London.

BEREND, D., and J. PAROUSH (1998): "When is the Condorcet's Jury Theorem Valid?," *Social Choice and Welfare*, 15, 481– 488.

BERG, S. (1993): "Condorcet's Jury Theorem, Dependency among Jurors," *Social Choice and Welfare*, 10, 87–95.

BERNHOLZ, P., and F. BREYER (1993): *Grundlagen der Politischen Ökonomie.* Mohr.

BLACK, D. (1958): *The Theory of Committees and Elections.* Cambridge University Press, Cambridge, MA.

BRAMS, S., and A. TAYLOR (1996): *Fair Division: From Cake-Cutting to Dispute Resolution.* Cambridge University Press, Cambridge, UK.

BUCHANAN, J. (1991): *Constitutional Economics.* Basil Blackwell, Oxford.

——— (1998): "Majoritarian Logic," *Public Choice*, 97, 13–21.

BUCHANAN, J., and G. TULLOCK (1965): *The Calculus of Consent: Logical Foundations of Constitutional Democracy.* University of Michigan Press.

COOTER, R. D. (2000): *The Strategic Consitution.* Princeton University Press, Princeton New Jersey.

D'ASPREMONT, C., and L. GÉRARD-VERET (1979): "Incentives and Incomplete Information," *Journal of Public Economics*, 11, 25–45.

DOWNS, A. (1957): *An Economic Theory of Democracy.* Harper and Row, New York.

EPPLE, D., and M. RIORDAN (1987): "Cooperation and Punishment under Repeated Majority Voting," *Public Choice*, 55, 41–73.

EPSTEIN, R. (1995): *Simple Rules for a Complex World.* Harvard University Press, Cambridge, Mass.

ERLENMAIER, U., and H. GERSBACH (2001): "Flexible Majority Rules," http://papers.ssrn.com/abstract=205829.

——— (2004): "Bundling and the Unanimity Rule," *CEPR Discussion Paper.*

FEDDERSEN, T., and W. PESENDORFER (1994): "Voting Behavior and Information Aggregation in Elections with Private Information," *Econometrica*, 65, 1029–1058.

——— (1996): "The Swing Voter's Curse," *American Economic Review*, 86, 408–424.

FELD, L., and G. KIRCHGÄSSNER (1998): "Die politische Ökonomie der direkten Demokratie: Eine Übersicht," *Discussion Paper, University of St. Gallen*, 9807.

FEREJOHN, J., M. FIORINA, and R. MCKELVEY (1987): "Sophisticated Voting and Agenda Independence in the Distributive Politics Setting," *American Journal of Political Science*, 31, 169–193.

FOLEY, D. (1967): "Resource Allocation and the Public Sector," *Yale Economic Essays*, 7(1), 45–98.

FUDENBERG, D., and J. TIROLE (1992): *Game Theory.* MIT Press, Cambridge, MA.

GERSBACH, H. (2002): "Democratic Mechanisms: Double Majority Rules and Flexible Agenda Costs," *Cesifo Working Paper*, 749.

——— (2004a): "Dividing Resources by Flexible Majority Rules," *Social Choice and Welfare.*

——— (2004b): "Fiscal Constitutions," *Constitutional Economics*, 15(1), 3–25.

——— (2004c): "Why One Person One Vote?," *Social Choice and Welfare, forthcoming.*

Gersbach, H., and B. Pachl (2004): "Flexible Majority Rules for Central Banks," *CEPR Discussion Paper*, 4398.

Gilligan, T., and K. Krehbiel (1987): "Collective Decision-Making and Standing Committees: An Informational Rationale for Restrictive Amendment Procedures," *Journal of Law, Economics, and Organization*, 3, 287–335.

Guttman, J. (1998): "Unanimity and Majority Rule: The Calculus of Consent Reconsidered," *European Journal of Political Economy*, 14, 189–207.

Harrington, J. J. (1986): "A Noncooperative Bargaining Game with Risk-Averse Players and an Uncertain Finite Horizon," *Economics Letters*, 20, 9–13.

——— (1990): "The Role of Risk Preferences in Bargaining when Acceptance of a Proposal Requires Less than Unanimous Approval," *Journal of Risk and Uncertainty*, 3, 135–154.

Harsanyi, J. (1955): "Cardinal Welfare, Individual Ethics and Interpersonal Comparability of Utility," *Journal of Political Economy*, 61, 309–321.

Herrero, M. (1985): *A Strategic Bargaining Approach to Market Institutions.* Ph.D. Dissertation, University of London.

Kolm, S. (1972): *Justice et Equité.* Paris: Edition du CNRS.

Koray, S. (2000): "Self-Selective Social Choice Functions Verify Arrow and Gibbard-Satterthwaite Theorems," *Econometrica*, 68(4), 981–995.

Ladha, K. (1992): "The Condorcet Jury Theorem, Free Speech, and Correlated Votes," *American Journal of Political Science*, 36, 617–634.

Lindahl, E. (1958): "Just Taxation — A Positive Solution," in *Classics in the Theory of Public Finance*, ed. by R. Musgrave, and A. Peacoc. Macmillian, translated from German.

May, K. (1952): "A Set of Independent, Necessary and Sufficient Conditions for Simple Majority Decisions," *Econometrica*, 20(4), 680–684.

Moore, J. (1992): "Implementation, Contracts, and Renegotiation in Environments with Complete Information," in *Advances in Economic Theory*, ed. by J. Laffont, pp. 182–282. Cambridge University Press, Cambridge,MA.

Moulin, H. (1981): "The Proportional Veto Principle," *Review of Economic Studies*, 48, 407–416.

——— (1995): *Cooperative Microeconomics: A Game-Theoretic Introduction.* Princeton.

Mueller, D. (1978): "Voting by Veto," *Journal of Public Economics*, 10, 57–75.

——— (1989): *Public Choice II.* Cambridge University Press, Cambridge.

MYERSON, R., and M. SATTERTHWAITE (1983): "Efficient Mechanisms of Bilateral Trading," *Journal of Economic Theory*, 29, 265–281.

ORDESHOOK, P. (1986): *Game Theory and Political Theory*. Cambridge University Press, Cambridge.

PIKETTY, T. (1999): "The Information Aggregation Approach to Political Institutions," *European Economic Review*, 43, 791–800.

RIKER, W. H. (1962): *The Theory of Political Coalitions*. Yale University Press, New Haven.

ROBERTSON, J., and W. WEBB (1998): *Cake-Cutting Algorithms: Be Fair If You Can*. Natick, MA: A. K. Peters.

ROUSSEAU, J. (1763): *The Social Contract and Discourses*. Everyman's Library, London.

SAARI, D. (1995): *Basic Geometry of Voting*. Springer-Verlag, Berlin.

SAMUELSON, P. (1969): "Pure Theory of Public Expenditure and Taxation," *Public Economics*, pp. 98–123.

SAUNDERS, C. (2001): *The Parliament as Partner: A Century of Constitutional Review*, vol. 12. University of Melbourne Law School, Public Law Research Paper.

SCHELLING, T. (1960): *Strategy of Conflict*. Cambridge, MA: Harvard University Press.

SCHOFIELD, N. (1972): "Is Majority Rule Special?," in *Probability Models of Collective Decision Making*, ed. by R. Niemi, and H. Weisberg. Merill Publishing, Columbus, Ohio.

SCHWARTZ, T. (1986): *The Logic of Collective Choice*. Columbia University Press, New York.

SEN, A. (1970): *Collective Choice and Social Welfare*. Holden-Day, San Francisco.

SHEPSLE, K. (1979): "Institutional Arrangements and Equilibrium in Multidimensional Voting Models," *American Journal of Political Science*, 23, 27–59.

VARIAN, H. (1974): "Equity, Envy and Efficiency," *Journal of Economic Theory*, 29(2), 217–244.

WALKER, C., and Y. AKDENIZ (eds.) (1997): *Virtual Democracy*, presented at the JETAI Conference, University of Glasgow.

WEINGAST, B. (1979): "A Rational Choice Perspective on Congressional Norm," *American Journal of Political Science*, 23, 245–262.

WICKSELL, K. (1896): *A New Principle of Just Taxation*. New York, St. Martin's Press.

YOUNG, H., and A. LEVENGLICK (1978): "A Consistent Extension of Condorcet's Election Principle," *SIAM Journal of Applied Mathematics*, 35(C), 283–300.